AIDS and the Law of
Workplace Discrimination

AIDS and the Law of Workplace Discrimination

Jeffrey A. Mello

Westview Press

BOULDER • SAN FRANCISCO • OXFORD

Copyright © 1995 by Westview Press, Inc.

Published in 1995 in the United States of America by Westview Press, Inc., 5500 Central Avenue, Boulder, Colorado 80301-2877, and in the United Kingdom by Westview Press, 36 Lonsdale Road, Summertown, Oxford OX2 7EW

Library of Congress Cataloging-in-Publication Data
Mello, Jeffrey A.
   AIDS and the law of workplace discrimination / by Jeffrey A. Mello.
      p.   cm.
   Includes bibliographical references and index.
   ISBN 0-8133-2295-2
   1. AIDS (Disease)—Patients—Employment—Law and legislation—United States.   2. Discrimination in employment—Law and legislation—United States.   I. Title.
KF3470.M45   1995
344.73'01133—dc20
[347.3041133]
                                                        94-29703
                                                        CIP

Printed and bound in the United States of America

The paper used in this publication meets the requirements of the American National Standard for Permanence of Paper for Printed Library Materials Z39.48-1984.

10   9   8   7   6   5   4   3   2   1

Contents

1

Introduction

The Problem

The public health epidemic surrounding the human immunodeficiency virus has become a harsh reality of life for both our nation and the world, permeating and reweaving the social fabric of our society in profound ways. The sharp societal differences in perceptions concerning public health, ethics, and civil liberties have created the largest body of legal cases attributable to a single disease in the history of American jurisprudence. AIDS, as a disease, is highly misunderstood. It affects many individuals in society who are already discriminated against due to their national origin, sexual orientation, substance abuse problems, or other medical condition such as hemophilia.

In addition to violations of individual liberties and, in some cases, civil rights, discrimination against those infected with HIV has broader public policy implications. The Presidential Commission on the HIV epidemic has concluded that "discrimination is impairing this nation's ability to limit the spread of the epidemic." While the United States Public Health Service has developed a strategy of early identification of those infected with HIV to assist in treatment and limit the spread of the virus, the absence of adequate safeguards against discrimination has been seen as a factor that seriously undermines these efforts.

AIDS is different from other illnesses or ailments with which the medical community and general public have familiarity and knowledge, making the problem of how best to deal with those infected with the virus clearly unprecedented. In February, 1994 the United States Centers for Disease Control had estimated that 1 million Americans were carriers of the HIV virus. In addition, 339,250 Americans had been diagnosed with full-blown AIDS with 204,390 deaths having had occurred at that time. By comparison, 292,000 Americans were killed in World War II and 58,000 lost their lives in Vietnam.

What is now known as AIDS was essentially unknown to the medical community prior to 1980 when Dr. Michael Gottlieb of UCLA noticed that a patient had a strange array of symptoms, including a rare ailment known as pneumocystis carinii pneumonia, (PCP). He subsequently published a study concerning an outbreak of PCP in five homosexual men in Los Angeles. Upon publication of the study in 1981, the United States Centers for Disease Control in Atlanta began investigating reports of similarly unusual opportunistic infections occurring in New York City as well as some additional cases in Los Angeles. The first official reporting of what is now known as AIDS appeared in the June 5, 1981 edition of the CDC publication *Morbidity and Mortality Weekly Report*.

HIV and AIDS

This book will discuss both the human immunodeficiency virus, commonly referred to as HIV or the HIV virus, and the illness commonly known as AIDS, an acronym for Acquired Immune Deficiency Syndrome. The HIV virus generally results in an individual eventually developing the condition AIDS. AIDS, in turn, leaves an individual susceptible to contracting a lethal illness. No one has ever died from the HIV virus or from AIDS, per se, but from other medical complications that result from prolonged infection with the virus. Below is an explanation of how the human immunodeficiency virus functions within the human body.

Epidemiology

The human body fights off infection by a series of complicated processes which collectively make up the functions of the immune system. The internal processes of the immune system includes three sequential stages. First the body identifies any foreign agents that have entered it. The body then forms antibodies that fight the foreign agents. Finally, the immune system regulates the production of these antibodies when and where the foreign agents are detected.

Epidemiological theories about AIDS tend to center on the process of the regulation of the production of such antibodies or the third stage of the immune system response. Most scientists doing research in this area believe that a viral agent perhaps in combination with, or in the presence of, one or more other cofactors, attacks and destroys certain cells known as T-helper lymphocyte cells. These cells normally trigger the production of antibodies once foreign substances have been detected and initial antibodies manufactured. Hence, while the immune system allows the body to form antibodies to fight off the virus, it is unable to regulate the ongoing production of the antibodies to control the spread of the virus.

The condition called AIDS is known to be caused by a retrovirus. Upon its discovery in 1981, it was referred to as the human t-lymphotropic virus type III (HTLV-III). It attacks the body's immune system and leaves the individual vulnerable to "opportunistic" diseases that are unusual in the general population. Until 1986, the United States Centers for Disease Control and most members of the medical community used the term HTLV-III most frequently to describe the virus that leads to AIDS. In 1987, the CDC publication *Morbidity and Mortality Weekly Report* changed to the usage of the acronym HIV (human immunodeficiency virus) to describe the AIDS virus. In the body, the HIV retrovirus attaches itself to certain disease-fighting cells of the immune system and displaces the natural genetic material of these cells with its own genetic material. This process subverts the functioning of those cells, rendering them useless for their usual functions.

The most severe medical complication of HIV infection occurs when something causes these HIV-infected blood cells, known as T-4 Helper Lymphocytes, to begin rapid reproduction. Since the genetic material in the cells is actually that of HIV, the rapid reproduction produces a significant weakening of the body's immune system. These T-4 Lymphocytes, also referred to as T-cells, are white blood cells which produce the antibodies to fight off disease.

Once an individual becomes infected with HIV, the virus may remain dormant for months, or even years before dividing and attacking the T-cells. In other words, there is no standard incubation period from the time an individual is infected with HIV until (s)he begins to develop symptoms of immune system disfunction. However, once the T-cells are destroyed the individual's immune system goes into rapid failure as the body has virtually no defense against opportunistic infections that individuals with healthy immune systems fight off with little adverse effect.

In the early 1980s, researchers hypothesized that the viral agent was transmitted through blood contact as a result of sexual intercourse, transfusions, or shared use of needles by intravenous drug users. Current research indicates that there are only four ways that the disease is transmitted: through sexual contact that results in the exchange of blood or semen; through the sharing of intravenous drug needles; through blood transfusions; and through transmission from infected mother to an unborn child. While there have been some documented cases of individuals becoming infected in health care settings, these transmissions have involved the exchange of bodily fluids, generally through accidents or poorly sterilized medical equipment.

Medical experts have repeatedly stated that the contact of blood or other body fluids with intact skin does *not* pose a risk of transmitting the HIV virus. An individual must be directly exposed to infected blood or other body fluids through an opening in the skin for transmission to occur. Although the virus has been detected in tears and saliva, there are no reported cases of transmission from these body fluids. Concerning sexual contact, it is fully believed in the medical community that the virus can not be transmitted by such intimate contact such as kissing, including oral-genital kissing, unless there is broken tissue or through the sharing of personal hygiene products such as toothbrushes.

Once the individual begins to suffer full-blown AIDS the disease becomes progressively debilitating. Although it can fall into periods of remission, an analogy can be made to winning some battles while losing the war. The clinical illness starts with vague debilitating symptoms including drenching night sweats, sustained fevers, chronic diarrhea, and weight loss. Sometimes there is also generalized enlargement of the lymph glands, a condition known as lymphadenopathy. Some, but not all, individuals who start with these symptoms experience what is known as oral "thrush," a painful yeast infection of the inner mouth, which develops from or in conjunction with the above symptoms. While the above ailments are very unpleasant, the symptoms of severe, chronic AIDS are far more debilitating. They include pneumocystis carinii pneumonia, an uncommon and often lethal form of pneumonia, Karposi's sarcoma, a rare form of skin cancer, gastrointestinal disorders, neurological infections and impairments, brain lesions, and a variety of other opportunistic infections and tumors.

A blood test known as the Enzyme-Linked Immunosorbent Assay, or "ELISA," is used to determine exposure to the virus. This test detects the presence of the HIV antibodies which develop in a person's blood up to six months after exposure to the HIV virus. Because of some reliability problems with the ELISA test, another more expensive and complicated but more accurate test known as the Western Blot, has been recommended and utilized to confirm the presence of antibodies. Individuals taking the HIV antibody tests and health official administering the tests have been warned that the tests only determine exposure to the HIV virus and not whether a person has or will ever develop the disease AIDS. However, it is believed that most, if not all, of those infected with HIV will eventually develop full-blown AIDS. For those who have been exposed to the virus, it has been estimated that 20-30% will develop mild symptoms of the disease within five years from the time of exposure and that 19% of those who develop such mild symptoms will progress to full-blown AIDS within 15-30 months from the onset of symptoms.

Once an individual develops the symptoms of full-blown AIDS, deterioration tends to be rapid. The severely weakened immune systems of those with full-blown AIDS usually results in death within twelve months of the onset of symptoms. A recent study of persons with AIDS in San Francisco, conducted between 1981 and 1988, reported an estimated median survival of all study patients of 12.5 months, an estimated three-year survival rate of 8.7%, and a five-year survival rate of only 3.4%

(Lemp, Payne, Neal, Temelso, & Rutherford, 1990). While newer treatments and therapies are continuously being developed and tested that may extend the lives of those with full-blown AIDS or delay the onset of symptoms for those already infected, the long-term prognosis for those with symptoms of the full-blown disease remains bleak.

There is no known cure for AIDS or any way to reverse the incidence of infection with the viral agent that contributes to the AIDS condition. Only a major breakthrough in medical research involving a method of stimulating the manufacture of new T-helper lymphocytes or a method of artificially simulating the working function of these lymphocytes is believed to be a potential effective treatment.

HIV Infection in the Workplace

Public health officials have asserted that current theories about HIV infection and its epidemiology are not consistent with the possibility of transmission through the kind of casual contact that occurs in a typical workplace. The Centers for Disease Control has reported that "medical researchers have isolated the HIV virus from blood, semen, saliva, tears, breast milk and urine...but epidemiological evidence has implicated only blood and semen in transmission...casual contact with saliva and tears does not transmit the infection...nor is it transmitted by contaminated food or water, air-borne or fecal-oral routes."

People infected with HIV have traditionally been grouped into one of four categories.

- Category I consists of those who have tested positive for exposure to the virus but have no physical symptoms of illness.

- Category II consists of those who have experienced mild symptoms of the disease AIDS. These previously-noted symptoms are considered "warning signs." Individuals with the symptoms are often said to be in a state of "pre-AIDS" and suffer from what is called AIDS-Related Complex, more commonly referred to by the acronym ARC.

- Category III consists of those who have the stronger symptoms of the disease AIDS, as previously noted. While an opportunistic infection has been contracted, hospitalization is usually not required and the individual remains able to work and carry on everyday life activities.

- Category IV consists of those who have full-blown AIDS and require hospitalization and/or personal assistance and are unable to work or care for themselves.

Individuals in the first three categories have all been the targets of discrimination in the workplace. People in categories II and III tend to experience the most serious and blatant discrimination based on fear of transmission while those in category I face discrimination that has to do more with perceptions involving the means by which they were infected.

These four categories should be extended to include yet another category. This category involves those who have no known HIV-infection but, due to their association with or membership in a known risk group, suffer discrimination based on others' fears of contracting the virus themselves and/or spreading it. As a result, it is necessary to expand the typologies to include this group of individuals who are members of or associated with high-risk groups. These revised typologies consist of Category I; members or associates of high-risk groups, Category II; asymptomatic carriers of the virus, Category III; individuals suffering from ARC, Category IV; persons with AIDS who are ambulatory and physically able to work, and Category V; persons with AIDS who are physically and/or mentally incapacitated. A caveat is in order here in that while the categories appear clearly defined and mutually exclusive, the symptoms and progressions of the disease are not necessarily linear. Individuals can and do enter into periods of remission over time, hence changing their categorical classification.

It should be noted that nowhere in this discussion has the term "victim" been employed. In the early stages of the epidemic, those with full-blown AIDS were frequently referred to as AIDS victims. The term "victim" is often used in medical practice and alludes to how debilitating and helpless those with the full-blown symptoms of HIV infection actually become. In more recent years, those with full-blown symptoms of AIDS prefer to call themselves and be referred to as "person with AIDS," often abbreviated to the acronym "PWA." These individuals see themselves not as victims but as those who are challenged by their condition. They often describe themselves as "living with AIDS," stressing the fact that they are still very much alive and engage in the same life activities they would be participating in if not infected. To them, the term "victim" is dehumanizing and fails to emphasize the strength of individuals living with and fighting against the disease. Further, some people with AIDS, such as those infected through blood transfusions or medical accidents, are often referred to in the media as "innocent victims." Such a nomenclature implies that there are some "guilty victims" who are deserving of their illness and fate.

Purpose of This Book

These terminologies and the common misconceptions that exist concerning HIV infection can be confusing. In media accounts, the acronym

AIDS may refer to anything from the production of antibodies to a fatal and highly contagious disease. Many employers, confused by such terminology, flatly refuse to hire any applicant who suffers from AIDS, no matter which stage of the disease afflicts the individual. Individuals who fall into categories I, II, III, and IV have shown over the course of the epidemic that they can be capable of adequate job performance. Clearly, those in the less symptomatic categories will tend to have the highest propensity and capacity for work. Ironically, however, those in the less-afflicted classes may be in the greatest need of protection from employment discrimination.

As a result, the purpose of this book is two-fold. First, it examines the federal and state laws that protect handicapped/disabled workers from employment discrimination and determines the extent to which these laws are able to protect individuals infected with the various classifications of HIV infection. A discussion will follow that addresses the efficacy of the current legal framework.

The second purpose is to forecast trends in employment discrimination law that can be expected to continue and escalate. HIV infection is changing. It is becoming more "mainstream," no longer affecting just those individuals who are members of "fringe" groups of society. Those infected with HIV are living longer throughout each of the various stages of their disease. These same individuals are becoming more vocal and activist about their illness. Societal and medical changes will certainly impact the state of how HIV infection is treated within the legal framework of employment law. In the light of the trends, recommendations for public policy initiatives will follow.

Foundation

At the foundation of this study is an analysis of the major court decisions that involve employment discrimination based on HIV infection or other medical conditions (such as tuberculosis) where the decision has been applied to a case involving HIV. A comprehensive presentation of this body of law is presented in Chapter 2. In sum, while many courts view HIV as a handicap under federal handicap discrimination law, there are questions and issues that are still unresolved. The HIV virus is a medical condition like no other ever known by the medical or legal communities. New aspects of the disease continue to be discovered so clear precedents have yet to be fully established. There are different classifications of the disease and the disease manifests itself quite differently in different individuals. Therefore clear legal precedents concerning employment discrimination relative to HIV remain somewhat elusive and undeveloped.

Significance

The significance of this study is that it will extend previous research in three ways. First, it will analyze and summarize all reported cases that have been heard by courts or commissions regarding employment discrimination and HIV. Previous commentary has had a much limited focus, generally looking at one landmark case and interpreting it within the parameters of HIV infection. Second, the study will specifically classify all of these cases utilizing the various categories of HIV infection. To date no work has yet done that systematically. Research that has been done concerning the legal issues surrounding the employment of those infected with HIV has not distinguished among the various classifications of HIV infection. While these typologies have been utilized in other areas of HIV-related research, notably medical research, they have not been extended to the study of employment discrimination. In addition, little attention has been paid to those who are not necessarily infected but are members of, or perceived to be members of, high-risk groups. As will be illustrated, these individuals are provided with some protection against handicap discrimination in employment under federal and some state laws.

Finally, this study will determine the extent to which existing laws are able to prevent such discrimination. Previous work generally makes conjectures or generalizations with limited data consisting of one, or in some cases, a few court cases. Only by comparing and contrasting decisions and examining an exhaustive number of cases can a more valid determination be made of the efficacy of existing laws in dealing with such discrimination.

Questions

This study will attempt to answer three critical questions:

1. The first is the extent to which HIV infection or the perception of HIV infection is a handicapping condition under federal employment law. This will be determined by analyzing the rulings of the courts and how the courts' interpretation of the law's definition of "handicapped" has been applied to HIV infection.

2. The second question is whether different classifications of HIV infection are judged differently. The extent to which courts distinguish or fail to distinguish the different categories of HIV infection in their rulings can have significant implications for a disease that has cyclical patterns of infection and progression.

3. The third question is whether existing laws protecting the handicapped from employment discrimination adequately cover HIV

infection. This will be answered by looking at successful employer defenses, the legal and theoretical foundations upon which these defenses are built, and the extent to which different courts interpret identical existing laws in a consistent manner.

Methodology

Scope

This investigation will focus on general work settings, excluding specialized segmented analysis of specific settings such as health care institutions, correctional institutions, etc.. The goal of this study is to examine laws that are general in that they apply to all work settings since there is no body of law that applies to specific work settings such as health care institutions, food service operations, or prisons. Professional associations of these specific work settings sometimes in conjunction with public health officials do issue general precautionary guidelines. Generally, workers in these professions find that the risk of being exposed to bodily fluids that may contain the HIV virus can be greatly reduced with simple precautions. Even health care settings, which would appear to produce some of the riskiest situations, are a work environment in which HIV is exceeding hard to transmit. The risks to health care professionals who take precautionary measures have been found to be remote even for those involved in invasive procedures. Nonetheless, an emergency medical technician is clearly at greater risk than an accountant or a computer operator. Therefore, special attention will be paid to court decisions that consider the specific nature of job responsibilities in reaching their conclusions.

Data Sources

The data used in this study consists of all cases involving HIV-related employment discrimination that have been heard and all complaints filed before federal and state courts and local human rights commissions since the beginning of the epidemic. While the study is primarily concerned with an examination of federal law, the inclusion of cases involving state courts and local human rights commissions is important for two reasons. First, many state and municipal laws are patterned after federal law. This is particularly true for laws relating to employment discrimination of the handicapped. While the decisions of these lower courts and agencies are certainly not binding legal precedent at the federal level, they provide some insights into how newer cases and statutory terminology might be interpreted. Secondly, these lower cases provide some key insights into some of the more pressing issues surrounding the HIV epidemic. State and municipal laws tend to be more responsive to social issues and problems than federal laws are with local laws usually promulgated well before their federal counterparts.

Two caveats are important in considering the nature of the data. Because the data utilized consists of cases that have gone to court, it may possibly cover only a portion of those individuals who are experiencing employment discrimination. Individuals who feel that the complaint process is too tiring, time consuming, expensive, or fraught with bureaucratic hurdles or corruption are less likely to register and pursue a complaint.

In addition, other cases of discrimination might involve out-of-court settlements by the parties. The majority of these cases are not published either in legal reporters or computerized data bases, although those that have been published have been included in this study. Exclusion of these unpublished out-of court settlements clearly limits our understanding of the nature and extent of HIV-related employment discrimination. However, these cases are not fully relevant to this study because it is designed to look at the judicial interpretation of existing laws.

Data Analysis

Data analysis first involved classifying all of the court cases into one of four categories of HIV status; high-risk group member, asymptomatic HIV-positive, ARC, or AIDS with the ability to work . Each category was then exhaustively examined by looking at the full legal text of the decisions in the legal reporters in which they appeared to determine the major legal concepts of handicapped employment discrimination law that were applied. Some legal concepts consisted of the grounds on which the suit was based, the legal principles on which it was decided, the definitions assigned to ambiguous statutory terms, etc. Next a legal framework was developed for each category of HIV status. This framework determines the extent to which each classification constitutes a handicap, areas of "gray" where the courts disagree, and the extent to which employers may legally discriminate under existing law. After developing a framework for each classification, the categories were then combined into one overall model of HIV-related employment discrimination. This model is used to determine how the legal issues and concepts are similar and different across different classifications.

Each case was then categorized using the following nine variables:

- level of law (federal, state, municipal)
- HIV status of employee (high risk group member, asymptomatic HIV-positive, ARC, AIDS)

- gender of employee
- type of discrimination (termination, denial of benefits, reassignment, refusal to hire, etc.)
- geographic region (federal court district in which case was heard)
- verdict renderer (judge, jury, commission or agency)
- judgment (employer, employee, out-of-court settlement)
- industry of employer (health care, government, education, food service, etc.)
- year verdict rendered

Bivariate cross-classification tables were prepared to examine whether any significant relationships existed between certain pairs of variables. Nine hypothesized relationships were developed and tested. They are as follows:

Hypothesis #1	Ho: Those in the more advanced stages of HIV infection are more likely to receive a ruling in their favor.
Hypothesis #2	Ho: State and local cases are more likely than federal cases to result in a ruling favoring the employee.
Hypothesis #3	Ho: The more severe the consequences for the plaintiff employee (i.e. termination or denial of benefits vs. reassignment or restrictions on job duties), the more likely the verdict will favor him/her.
Hypothesis #4	Ho: Commissions and agencies are more likely than judges to render verdicts for employees.
Hypothesis #5	Ho: Those in more advanced stages of HIV infection are more likely to receive more severe forms of discrimination (i.e. termination or denial of benefits vs. reassignment or restrictions on job duties).
Hypothesis #6	Ho: Judgment is more likely to be rendered for the employer in industries such as health care and food service with a higher *perceived* potential for transmission due to the presence of bodily fluids and fears of food contamination.

Hypothesis #7	Ho: As time has progressed, it has become more likely that a greater percentage of cases will be judged in favor of the employee.
Hypothesis #8	Ho: Cases heard in the northeastern and far western United States are more likely than cases heard in other areas, particularly the deep South, to favor the employee.
Hypothesis #9	Ho: When the plaintiff employee is a woman, the verdict is more likely to be issued in her favor.

The results of these hypotheses tests provide insightful information toward understanding HIV-related employment discrimination that is critical to gaining a more complete understanding of the different elements of the phenomenon. Variations in judgment of cases relative to level of law, category of discrimination, verdict renderer, industry, time, gender and geographic region reveal vital relationships that shed additional light on how the law actually functions relative to HIV-related employment discrimination. The data is also utilized to develop a frame work within which to examine the issue from a socio-legal perspective. An analysis of type of discrimination relative to HIV status, industry, time, gender and geographic region assists in understanding HIV-related employment discrimination from a macrosocial perspective which facilitates a discussion of the implications the study has for both law and public policy and employers and company policy.

Implications and Presentation of Results

Implications

On a micro level, this study is designed to illuminate conflicts between employees and their employers. It is a study in management and organizational behavior that focuses on employee relations and employment law. On a macro level, the study analyzes conflicts of societal values, legal principles, and public health policies that are likely to continue to emerge in the future, requiring resolution involving interest groups, policymakers, health officials, and the court system.

This study has numerous implications for law and public policy. They include the sufficiency of existing laws concerning discrimination based on handicap status and the extent to which private enterprises deal with societal problems within their own organization without government intervention. The study also analyzes how the court system deals with a social problem that clearly could not have been anticipated when applicable/relevant laws that have been applied to it were developed. As the societal problems associated with AIDS inevitably will escalate, the legal framework developed in this study is designed to facilitate a discussion of both public policy issues and managerial responsibilities relative to HIV.

Presentation of Results

Chapter 2 provides the legal framework within which employment discrimination based on HIV status is grounded. An awareness of the development of this framework from both philosophical and operational perspectives is key to understanding many of the court decisions that have been rendered and are discussed within subsequent chapters.

Chapter 3 presents an analysis of all reported employment discrimination cases based on HIV status since the beginning of the epidemic. This chapter consists of four sections, one presented for each of the four categories in which an individual maintains the ability to work (high-risk group member, asymptomatic carrier of HIV, person with ARC, and person with AIDS who maintains the ability to work). The framework developed is designed to illustrate the extent to which individuals in each of the four categories find protection from employment discrimination under existing handicap discrimination laws.

Chapter 4 presents an analysis across categories of the major ways employers have discriminated relative to HIV status. Cases are grouped together according to the means the employer has used to discriminate (specific employer behaviors), regardless of the category of HIV infection. Through this analysis a determination is made concerning the consistency of applicability of laws which protect those infected with HIV across categories of HIV infection. The objective is to present a systematic model of precedent-setting cases concerning specific employer behaviors that allegedly discriminate and the legal consequences of these behaviors, as determined by the court's interpretations of them.

Chapter 5 examines the defense strategies employers have used when faced with discrimination charges. Presented is an analysis of the extent to which the courts have validated specific defenses and an analysis of their legal justifications. This discussion illustrates the success or failure of employers to have discrimination charges dismissed regardless of the specific discriminatory behaviors engaged in.

Chapter 6 presents the quantitative analysis of the hypothesized relationships between variables in the cases. Upon presentation of each of the nine hypotheses and the statistical data used to test them, the significance of each relationship is discussed along with any implications the relationships has for understanding the phenomena of HIV-related employment discrimination.

The concluding chapter, Chapter 7, examines the adequacies and inadequacies of existing laws, as reflected in the analyses presented in the preceding chapters. Recommendations for legal and policy initiatives are provided and, given that such initiatives will take time to develop and implement, the implications of the existing legal framework for organizations is discussed. Incorporated within this discussion are recommendations concerning how employers and employees might best deal with HIV issues in the workplace.

2

The Legal Framework
and Its Evolution

Throughout the course of this discussion, the terms HIV and AIDS are used somewhat liberally and interchangeably. It is important for the reader to remember that HIV infection is a causal factor in the condition known as AIDS. However, HIV infection is not synonymous with AIDS nor does it signify any illness or immune system suppression in and of itself. In several instances in this chapter the term AIDS is utilized where HIV might have been more appropriate. The reason for this is that much, if not most, prior research, fails to distinguish among the categorical classifications of HIV infection relative to employment law. Although medical research has generally been precise in its terminology, legal scholarship has been a bit sloppy in generalizing the conditions associated with HIV infection. While a major objective of this study is to correct this limitation of legal scholarship, it is critical to keep in mind that much of the developmental framework presented within does not distinguish among asymptomatic infection, ARC, and full-blown AIDS.

Background

Throughout the course of civilization, illnesses, particularly those caused by disease, have been met with prejudice and discrimination. In Biblical times, for example, the leper was shunned by society and treated as an outcast. During the Middle Ages, the arrival of the Black Plague was met with violent social upheaval and resulted in persecution of Jews. Early in the 20th century, prostitutes thought to be infected with venereal diseases were quarantined. In the present day, those afflicted with Acquired Immune Deficiency Syndrome (AIDS) are frequently the victims of a deadly and misunderstood disease. They are also subject to cruel, unjustified discrimination in many aspects of their lives. Indeed, modern day comparisons have been made between AIDS and leprosy. Society obviously seems to have made very little, if any, progress in terms of its understanding of unfamiliar diseases or its tolerance for those afflicted with such ailments.

then

The Nature and Extent of HIV-Related Discrimination

The fact that people with AIDS are often looked down upon is probably not surprising when one considers with whom the virus began and still most frequently strikes. The HIV virus that causes AIDS initially inflicted individuals who were already members of marginal social groups. Members of the gay community and intravenous drug users were often considered to be living on the fringes of society. Many members of society stigmatized, if not ostracized them for their sexual practices or drug use patterns.

These factors were complicated by a lack of knowledge concerning how the virus was transmitted, resulting in substantial numbers of people fearing the chance of catching an incurable and fatal disease through casual social contact. Further, many cultures consider blood and semen, the usual carriers of HIV infection, to be ritually polluting. It is not surprising that many individuals in society refused to believe that they could be personally affected by the disease and were indifferent to its impact on those afflicted with it.

A 1988 survey of high school students conducted by the United States Centers for Disease Control found that this group knew very little about AIDS. For example, fewer than 60% knew that the virus could not be transmitted by public toilets, fewer than 40% knew that transmission via insect bites was impossible, and 10% believed that the virus could be transmitted through a handshake. It seems likely that their parents, teachers, and other adults may have influenced many of these beliefs and values through their own biases.

Ignorance and public hostility toward people with AIDS is extensive and continues to run rampant. This was reflected in a survey conducted by the Harvard University School of Public Health (Blendon & Donelan, 1988). The results showed that 81% of those surveyed felt public identification of infected persons should take priority over the individual's right to privacy. Twenty-five percent said that they would refuse to work alongside an infected coworker. Eleven percent fully believed that they could be infected with the virus by working alongside someone who was a carrier. Twenty-nine percent favored a policy of tattooing those known to carry the virus. Seventeen percent supported banishing those with AIDS to islands or other isolated locales. Thirty percent believed that those with AIDS should be isolated from others in both work and school settings. Twenty-two percent believed that those afflicted with AIDS were "getting their rightful due."

Given that discrimination is largely a by-product of ignorance and fear, education might appear to be one attitudinal remedy. Teaching a society about HIV and AIDS is a challenge but some progress has been made. In many larger cities, where most of the highest concentrations of populations with HIV and AIDS are located, a number of education efforts have been quite successful. Educators in Los Angeles, San Francisco, and New York have all reported that prejudices against people with AIDS can be dramatically reduced with education. Other efforts aimed at groups in controlled social settings such as the workplace have also met with success. Despite some of these successes, the immense and irrational fear of AIDS can often block comprehension of the most basic medical facts.

The anxiety surrounding AIDS can, in part, be traced to five major areas of fear or discomfort shared by many members of society; a discomfort surrounding issues of human sexuality, the fear of being stigmatized, the fear of being helpless, the discomfort surrounding mental illness, and the fear and discomfort concerning issues of death. Hence, we can see that dealing with the social aspects of AIDS is fraught with complexities and anxieties that extend into many other areas of life and culture. It is quite likely that irrational fears about AIDS will continue to flourish even with the presence of good educational programs, strong factual information, and credible sources of such information. Education efforts geared toward attitudinal change may not be enough. As a result, the responsibility must fall on legislative authorities and public policy makers, such as public health and human service officials, to provide and develop an effective means of dealing with AIDS-based discrimination in our society.

There is no doubt that AIDS concerns have permeated the corporate world. A recent survey found that of domestic firms with over 5,000 employees, 75% had had employee cases of AIDS, with the average being six occurrences. Of firms with over 10,000 employees, 90% had had at least one case. The workplace mirrors many of society's attitudes towards AIDS as those with AIDS, or perceived to be at risk for AIDS, experience discrimination in all areas of their lives, including employment opportunities.

There have been numerous incidents in which employees afflicted with AIDS suffered discrimination. In one case, an employer refused to take back an employee who had been diagnosed with early symptoms of the disease while on a leave of absence. In another case a known homosexual was fired when he took a day off from work to see his doctor. It was assumed that the employee had AIDS. An airline flight attendant was fired because it was assumed that his visibly swollen glands were due to an HIV-related infection. It appears that when faced with the possibility of losing the business of customers and/or losing the services of current or potential employees due to fears concerning an employee or coworker who had AIDS, the most common employer reaction has been to fire the employee who has or is even suspected of having AIDS. Other employers have transferred an infected employee to an isolated work area or have placed the employee on indefinite sick leave.

While some have argued against AIDS-related employment discrimination from a moral perspective, others have argued against it from an economic perspective. Employment discrimination toward those with AIDS can be said to be inefficient because it squanders the organization's investment in training and can result in direct decreases in production. The replacement of a worker generally results in a period of diminished productivity during the time it takes the newer employee to learn the job to the level of efficiency of the replaced employee. In addition, despite the fact that many employees may not feel comfortable working with an HIV-infected coworker, there may be some who are empathetic and/or unaffected by irrational fears of contagion. These coworkers who support their HIV-infected colleague can easily have their morale and attitude toward their employer damaged with a resulting negative effect on their own motivation and productivity.

Role of the Employment-at-Will Doctrine

One may wonder why our legal system allows an employer to arbitrarily dismiss or otherwise mistreat an employee afflicted with AIDS, or any other employee for that matter. The answer is employment-at-will, a doctrine that has constituted the common law concerning the employment relationship in the United States since the late 19th century. H.G. Wood first postulated the "at-will" doctrine in his *Treatise On the Law of Master and Servant* in 1877, stating that hiring of employees is for an indefinite duration and at the discretion of the employer. The employment relationship can be terminated at the will of either party for any or even no reason. Hence, the doctrine appears to be an extension of a laissez-faire philosophy of commerce calling for a free market economy with no government intervention. Free enterprise abhors government interference in both markets and decisions made by business owners. These decisions include whom to hire and the terms and conditions of employment.

The doctrine of employment-at-will first found significant support in the court system in 1884 in the case of Payne v. Western and Atlantic RA Co.. In that case a Tennessee court confirmed the right of an employer to hire or fire any individual for good cause, bad cause, or no cause at all. While the concept of employment-at-will may seem dated by today's labor standards, it was applied in the federal courts as recently as 1977 in a major case. In Clark v. Prentice Hall, Inc. the court held that a plaintiff's employment was terminable at will and that the employer, with or without cause and regardless of motive, could discharge an employee without liability. While the doctrine is designed to protect the privacy of the employment relationship for both the employer and employee, the utilization and citation of the doctrine has centered on the employer's right to terminate a worker rather than an employee's right to leave his/her job. Employment-at-will continues to be applied up to the present day in defense of many alleged discrimination cases.

It is misleading to infer that workers have no protection whatsoever from unscrupulous and unethical employers. Legislators at the federal level have made some dents in the employment-at-will doctrine. In 1935, passage of the National Labor Relations Act, also known as the Wagner Act, allowed labor unions through the collective bargaining agreement, to introduce into employment contracts the idea that employees could be fired only for just cause. Public sector employees have generally been protected by the courts in the application of Constitutional due process guarantees. These guarantees prohibit the government from discharging its employees without "just cause." Private sector, non-unionized employees, on the other hand, have very limited coverage. Overall, approximately 75% of the employees in the United States have no explicit protection from arbitrary dismissal under existing laws or contracts.

It should be noted however, that many state statutes allow recognized exceptions to the employment-at-will doctrine for terminations that violate a recognized public policy. Such findings of public policy violations are judicially manufactured and involve employer actions that are "contrary to public interest." The public policy exception is often referred to as "wrongful discharge" and has included employee terminations for whistleblowing, refusal to commit a crime, and absence due to jury duty. This concept of wrongful discharge is illustrated in the 1983 case of Goins v. Ford Motor Company. A Michigan court of appeals found that an employee terminated for filing a worker's compensation claim has judicial recourse because his termination is contrary to public policy.

An interesting point concerning the concept of wrongful discharge is its potential applicability to an employee with HIV. Arguably, an HIV-infected employee discharged solely because of his/her HIV status might have a claim for wrongful discharge on the theory that the termination violates public policy. Clearly, however, such an individual would stand a better change in his/her action against an employer if the firing violated a specific federal or state law.

Employment Discrimination and Federal Law

Establishment of Protected Classes

In recent years, the federal government and a number of state governments have enacted legislation prohibiting employment discrimination against certain classes of individuals in both the public and private sectors.

- Title VII of the Civil Rights Act of 1964 prohibits discrimination in employment based on race, color, religion, gender, or national origin. It covers employment terms and conditions such as selection, placement, promotion, discharge, training, and compensation.
- The Pregnancy Discrimination Act of 1978 protects pregnant women from unfair and unjust treatment as an amendment to the Title VII of the Civil Rights Act. As an amendment, the provisions and scope of the act are identical to those of Title VII.
- The Age Discrimination in Employment Act, passed in 1967 and amended in 1986, prohibits employment discrimination against job applicants and employees at or over the age of 40.

In all of these cases, however, the burden of proof falls on the employee to prove discrimination and to also prove that the discrimination is a result of the employee's membership in one of the above categories of a "protected class."

Handicapped Discrimination Law Application

Vocational Rehabilitation Act

In 1973 Congress passed the Vocational Rehabilitation Act. This act extended the rights of employees under Title VII of the Civil Rights Act to workers who were handicapped. According to its sponsor, Senator Humphrey, the Act's purpose, was an attempt "to share with handicapped Americans the opportunities for an education, transportation, housing, health care and jobs that other Americans take for granted." The Act has been called the "Bill of Rights for Handicapped Persons" as well as the "Civil Rights Act for the Handicapped" because of the protection and guarantees it offers to those with physical or mental disabilities.

In passing the Act, the Senate paid particular attention to two problems that hindered the handicapped in their lives. The first was that the handicapped were socially isolated due to a lack of access to adequate educational opportunities; the second, that the handicapped were largely unemployed or underemployed. It might seem that the paucity of educational opportunities contributed to unemployment. However, Congress recognized that discrimination, not a lack of training, prevented many handicapped persons from securing meaningful employment.

The Act is comprised of three subsections requiring employers subject to its provisions to provide equal employment opportunities to the handicapped. In other words, handicapped workers are to receive treatment and opportunities equal to those who are not handicapped. Section 501 of the act specifically prohibits employment discrimination against the handicapped by the federal government. Section 503 applies the same mandates to federal government contractors and subcontractors and Section 504 extends the coverage of the Act to all recipients of federal grants and funds.

Section 504 of the statute also specifically extends protection against discrimination to three different groups of individuals in its definition of what constitutes a "handicapped individual." It covers those who have "an actual physical or mental impairment which substantially limits one or more major life activities," those "with a record of physical or mental impairment which substantially limits one or more major life activities," and those "regarded as having a physical or mental impairment which substantially limits one or more major life activities." While the original version of the act, passed in 1973, was silent on what specifically constituted a "physical or mental impairment," the revised version of the act, as amended in 1982, describes a physical or mental impairment as "any physiological disorder or condition, cosmetic disfigurement, or anatomical loss affecting one or more of the following body systems; neurological; musculoskeletal; special sense organs; respiratory; genito-urinary; hemic and lymphatic; skin; and endocrine; or any mental or psychological disorder, such as mental retardation, organic brain syndrome, emotional or mental illness, and specific learning disabilities." Similarly, while the original act did not specifically classify "major life activities," the amended version defined them to be "functions such as caring for one's self, performing manual tasks, walking, seeing, hearing, speaking, breathing, learning, and working."

One of the more interesting aspects of the act was the broad definition of a handicapped person to include persons who suffer discrimination because of past handicaps that no longer exist (second category) or because of the perceptions and attitudes of others (third category). This second category, "having a record of such impairment," is distinguished from the first category, "having such impairment," in that under the former, a person no longer has to have a current physical or mental impairment to qualify. If an employer decides to terminate an employee based on the individual's past history of impairment or the fear that the condition will recur, the employee is protected under this part of the definition. As will be discussed, this distinction is important in cases involving HIV.

In an appendix to the act, the United States Department of Health and Human Services cites examples of some conditions that should qualify under such an interpretation of past impairments. These conditions include people with or with a history of mental or emotional illness, heart disease, or cancer who have since recovered as well as persons incorrectly classified of having a condition such as mental retardation.

The third category of handicapped, "regarded as having such an impairment," allows inclusion of a large number of individuals are not covered under the first two categories. These individuals have either a physical or mental impairment that does not substantially limit one or more major life activities or a physical or mental impairment that substantially limits a major life activity because *someone else* believes they are so limited. The United States Department of Health and Human Services also cited examples of some qualifying conditions under this category in the same appendix to the act. These conditions include persons with physical traits such as a limp or disfiguring scar. This distinction is also critical when applied to those with HIV.

Regardless of the three categories in which an individual might claim membership to define him/herself as handicapped under the statute, one important and somewhat controversial qualification exists. It involves the inclusion by Congress of the term "otherwise qualified." Section 504 of the Act, for example, states that "No otherwise qualified handicapped individual in the United States...shall, solely by reason of his or her handicap, be excluded from the participation in, be denied the benefits of, or be subjected to discrimination under any program or activity receiving federal financial assistance or under any program or activity conducted by any Executive agency or by the United States Postal Service." Section 503 likewise requires covered government contractors and subcontractors to take affirmative action to employ *"otherwise qualified"* handicapped individuals.

The distinction of "otherwise qualified" is an important one. It assumes that the individual is capable of performing the normal requirements of a job even through he/she is handicapped. In its first case constructing and interpreting the Section 504 nondiscrimination requirement, the United States Supreme Court made a landmark ruling that involved the qualification "otherwise qualified." In Southeastern Community College v. Davis, the Court held that a rejected applicant to a nursing school program who suffered a severe hearing impairment, while obviously handicapped, was not otherwise qualified because employment of a deaf nurse could present a danger to patients and fellow employees. While Davis was clearly not an employment case per se, its findings have implications for cases involving alleged employment discrimination. These implications follow from the fact that the decision was based on Davis' employability and the fact that her handicap was judged to impede her ability to perform the normal tasks associated with her job.

The Davis case set a critical precedent in that courts now had to decide whether a handicapped individual was otherwise qualified relative to his or her physical handicaps. Indeed, just two years later, a Federal Court of Appeals used the Davis decision to support its finding in the case of Prewitt v. United States Postal Service. The court supported the Davis ruling in finding that an "insurmountable barrier" handicap need not be redressed by an employer in this case. The applicant's handicap, which limited mobility in the left arm and shoulder, was so severe or limiting as to make him unqualified for the position, thus making any necessary accommodations by the employer unreasonable. Similarly, in Carni v. Metropolitan St. Louis Sewer District, both the district and appellate courts ruled that an employee who cannot perform job responsibilities receives no protection from Section 504.

As a result of the Davis ruling, under both Sections 503 and 504 of the Act, an individual charging an employer with discrimination based solely on the reasons of his/her handicap must not only establish that he/she satisfied the statutory definition of a "handicapped individual" but must also demonstrate that he or she is an "otherwise qualified" individual who meets all job requirements. The alleged victim of discrimination hence bears a two-fold burden of proof. In the event that an individual's handicap prevents him or her from satisfactorily performing a job, precedence established that the Rehabilitation Act will not protect the individual.

Under Section 503 (b) of the act, an individual charging an employer with discrimination is required to file a complaint with the United States Department of Labor's Office of Federal Contracts Compliance Program. Since the Rehabilitation Act provides such a specific legal remedy and procedure, courts have ruled that no private course of action is allowed. Indeed there have been no documented cases where individuals have been permitted to pursue a private course of action for violations of the Act. Given the cumbersome bureaucracy of most federal agencies, one must question the efficacy of such a process to remedy cases of alleged employment discrimination. To further question the efficacy of the statute in promoting opportunities for the handicapped, it is also critical to remember that the Act protects handicapped individuals against employment discrimination only if the employer is federally supported. It offers handicapped individuals no protection whatsoever from employment discrimination in the private sector.

The above discussion illustrates that although the Vocational Rehabilitation Act was designed to prevent discrimination based on handicap, there are a number of conditions that must be met to satisfy the provisions of the Act. The Davis, Prewitt, and Carni cases all illustrate situations in which individuals who the courts clearly found to be handicapped were not protected by the Act. At face value the above analysis of the terminology utilized in the Act and its interpretation by the courts left unresolved the question of whether HIV infection would be protected under the Act and, if it is so, the extent of the protection offered by the Act.

The issue of whether AIDS would fit within the 1973 Rehabilitation

Act's definition of a handicap was supported in two early non-AIDS cases. In the case of E. E. Black, Ltd. v. Marshall, a district court in Hawaii rejected the argument that the definition of "handicapped" in the statute was unconstitutionally vague. It ruled that "impairment" meant "any condition which weakens, diminishes, restricts or otherwise damages an individual's health or physical or mental activity." Under this definition, AIDS could clearly be interpreted as a handicap.

In the landmark 1985 case of Arline v. School Board of Nassau County, a Federal Court of Appeals ruled that a contagious disease, in this case, tuberculosis, constitutes a handicap under the Rehabilitation Act. In Arline, the plaintiff was dismissed from her position as a third grade school teacher because of her previous infection with tuberculosis. Arline had contracted the disease in 1957 after which it went into remission. She was hired by the School board in 1966 and was healthy until she suffered three relapses during 1977-1978 after which the school board dismissed her. The Arline ruling clearly stated that contagious diseases are protected under the Act as a handicapping condition.

While the ruling covered tuberculosis rather than AIDS, the case set a precedent for a broader interpretation of the Act's inclusion of contagious diseases under its coverage. Under this broader interpretation one could plausibly reach the conclusion that asymptomatic workers infected with a contagious virus, such as HIV, could be considered "handicapped" in the sense that infection could result in impairment of the major life activity of gainful employment. This situation would occur when infected individuals suffer adverse employment action as a result of their condition with or without physical manifestations of the disease. Since the case did not specifically address HIV, it obviously did not set direct precedent for an HIV-based discrimination suit. However, plausible connections between the two contagious diseases of tuberculosis and HIV were certainly presented.

The first major administrative law decision addressing AIDS in an employment context was Shuttleworth v. Broward County Office of Budget and Management Policy where the Florida Commission on Human Relations answered the specific question of whether AIDS constitutes a handicap. Shuttleworth, a state clerical worker, was fired from his job because he had contracted AIDS. He was found to be handicapped and protected under Florida state law. While the case was clearly not a Rehabilitation Act case, it was significant because the Florida anti-discrimination-in-employment statute defined a handicap exactly as did the Rehabilitation Act. In its decision, the Commission ruled that without positive proof of casual workplace transmission of the virus, the firing of an HIV-infected employee was unlawful. Shuttleworth eventually settled out of court for $190,000, attorney's fees, and reinstatement to a different position with the school board.

An interesting point concerning the Shuttleworth decision was that in reaching its verdict, the Commission cited the Eleventh Circuit's decision in Arline as it related to communicable diseases. However, the Arline case had been appealed to the United States Supreme Court, which subsequently agreed to hear and rule on it. A Supreme Court reversal of the Arline decision would have allowed Shuttleworth to be challenged and probably reversed. Shuttleworth and Arline became intertwined in this regard. The connection became closer when the Supreme Court, in its ruling on Arline, specifically addressed the issue of AIDS. This ruling is discussed below.

In a non-employment case that supported the Shuttleworth decision, the New York State Supreme Court ruled just two months later that AIDS was a physical impairment for the purposes of coverage under the Rehabilitation Act. In District 27 Community School Board v. Board of Education, the court ruled that the New York City Board of Education had properly allowed a student infected with HIV to attend and remain in a public school even though he showed clinically evidenced immune suppression but no physical symptoms of AIDS or ARC. The court held that automatic exclusion from school of children with AIDS or ARC who were asymptomatic violated the Rehabilitation Act. Neither Shuttleworth nor District 27 was binding legal precedent; Shuttleworth because it was based on state rather than federal law and District 27 because it did not cover employment discrimination. Both opinions are significant however, in that they recognize AIDS as a handicap to be a plausible judicial stance.

In another interpretation of HIV as a handicap, a Massachusetts Superior Court ruled in the 1986 case of Cronan v. New England Telephone Company that AIDS was a handicap under Massachusetts state law. In this case, a repair technician claimed that his physical condition, ARC, at the time, was a handicap. He asserted that his privacy had been invaded and civil rights violated when management of the company publicly announced the state of his health. Cronan's coworkers walked off the job and even threatened to lynch him. As a result, the employer suspended Cronan from his job. In an interpretation that looked at the issue from a perspective different than those of previous courts, the court ruled that "a person with AIDS is handicapped regardless of whether he is presently suffering any adverse physical effects of AIDS and that it was the *potential* to contract *other* illnesses that constituted the handicap." The major significance of this decision was that Massachusetts state anti-discrimination laws used the same language as the Rehabilitation Act to define the term "handicapped person." This decision reinforced the Florida court's interpretation and decision in the Shuttleworth case.

As we have seen, people infected with HIV, particularly in the earlier stages of infection, received some favorable treatment in initial court decisions. However, there was still much controversy concerning not only the disease itself but its various progressions and manifestations and the extent to which they were covered under Federal law.

1986 Department of Justice Opinion

The status of HIV as a handicapping condition changed abruptly on June 23, 1986 when the United States Department of Justice released a memorandum discussing the application of the Rehabilitation Act to those afflicted with AIDS. The memo stated, in part, that there is

> little difficulty concluding that the disabling effects of the disease on its victims qualify as handicaps...the effects of AIDS constitute impairment...AIDS is a physiological disorder or condition affecting the hemic and lymphatic systems and possibly affecting the brain and central nervous systems as well. This impairment substantially limits the major life activity of resisting disabling and ultimately fatal diseases and may directly cause brain damage and disorders. Moreover, it should be noted that AIDS by definition involves the presence of an opportunistic disease, such as pneumocystis carinii pneumonia, that frequently will entail substantial limitations on major life activities....Furthermore, if AIDS patients are believed to be substantially limited in their major life activities this would render them handicapped under the third statutory criterion of that term, i.e., being regarded as having a qualifying impairment.

While the Department of Justice opinion concluded that Section 504 of the Rehabilitation Act protected those with the *disabling effects* of AIDS and related conditions, it also concluded that an individual's real or perceived ability to transmit the disease to others is *not* a handicap within the meaning of the statute. It stated that "while the disabling effects of AIDS or ARC may be a substantial limitation on major life activities and therefore a handicap, the ability to transmit the disease to others is not a protected characteristic under Section 504." In this instance, discrimination based on a fear of contagion would not fall within the protection offered by Section 504. The Department arrived at this conclusion by apparently ignoring established medical opinions and giving credence to employers' irrational fears about workplace transmission of AIDS. As a result, employers would be able to discharge those suffering from AIDS not because of the disabling effects of the disease but from a fear of the employee's likelihood of transmitting the disease. Furthermore, this opinion implied that those testing HIV-positive without the disabling effects of the disease would have no protection against any discrimination by their employer.

In its opinion, the Department of Justice clearly did not consider the diminished physical capacity of a person with AIDS as a qualifying impairment under Section 504 of the Rehabilitation Act. Instead it defined the handicap as a defect in the immune system. This definition appeared to short-circuit the legal protection of Section 504 which requires a case-by-case analysis of the specifics of the condition and of the link between the condition and the ability to work before a determination of employability is made. In sum, the Justice Department memorandum implied that an employer could lawfully discriminate against people with AIDS or ARC if it did so out of fear of contagion rather than because of the disabling aspects of the disease.

Public health officials quickly responded to the Department of Justice's memorandum. In direct reaction to the opinion, the United States Public Health Service immediately reiterated its assertion that the AIDS virus was not transmitted by casual contact either in schools or the workplace. In support of the same contention, the American Medical Association filed an amicus brief with the Supreme Court for the upcoming Arline appeal case arguing that employers should not, as the Department of Justice suggested, be allowed to discriminate based on an irrational fear of the risk of casual transmission of the HIV virus.

Arline Appeal to the United States Supreme Court

Less than one year later, on March 3, 1987, the United States Supreme Court handed down its decision in Nassau County School Board v. Arline, affirming the decision of the Eleventh Circuit Court of Appeals. The ruling indicated that an individual with tuberculosis was not removed from coverage of Section 504 of the Vocational Rehabilitation Act. The Court specified that an employer must make reasonable accommodations to the employee and that one who is likely to transmit an infectious disease in the workplace "will not be otherwise qualified for his or her job if reasonable accommodation will not eliminate that risk." The decision further stated that a person who is both contagious and has either an existing impairment or a record of such impairment is handicapped under Section 504. This section stipulated that a contagious disease, in and of itself, did not appear to be a handicapping condition. Arline, in this case, fit the above qualification standards as she had a "record of impairment," having been hospitalized for tuberculosis some 20 years earlier.

The Supreme Court decision in Arline clearly established that, in general, contagious diseases are protected under Section 504. It also chose to address the question of whether AIDS would qualify as a handicap under 504, even though the Arline decision was not about AIDS. Rather than specifically answer the question of whether HIV-infection was covered, the court chose to state that its decision in the Arline case was not to be interpreted or applied to cases involving HIV or AIDS and that it was not addressing the issue of whether or not a carrier of AIDS qualifies for protection under Section 504 of the Rehabilitation Act in deciding the Arline case. In its ruling, the Court stated that "this case does not present, and we therefore do not reach, the questions whether a carrier of a contagious disease such as AIDS could be considered to have a physical impairment, or whether such a person could be considered, solely on the basis of contagiousness, a handicapped person as defined by the Act." Furthermore, while the Arline decision left open the question of whether a positive test result for HIV would, by itself, constitute an impairment, the stipulation of an existing impairment or a history of such impairment to accompany the contagious status appears to imply that asymptomatic carriers of the virus might fall outside of the protection of Section 504.

The Supreme Court's unwillingness to address HIV in the Arline case, or more appropriately, its willingness to avoid addressing HIV, maintained a lack of legal clarity. An Arline ruling that addressed HIV would have set critical legal precedent for how HIV was to be interpreted under the terms and definitions of the Rehabilitation Act. Although the Rehabilitation Act did not cover the majority of workplaces, its terminology was incorporated by many state laws. Hence, in considering the "reach" of the Act and court decisions rendered that interpreted it, the Act directly or indirectly covered a significant number of workers.

The Arline case also resulted in the Supreme Court placing a specific restriction on the employment of workers with handicaps. In its decision the Supreme Court explicitly narrowed the definition of a handicapped individual by stating that "only those individuals who are both handicapped and otherwise qualified are eligible for relief" under the Rehabilitation Act. The Court defined "otherwise qualified" in the following manner:

> a person who poses a significant risk of communicating an infectious disease to others in the workplace will not be otherwise qualified for his or her job if reasonable accommodation will not eliminate that risk. This standard requires the courts to use a balancing test, weighing the right of handicapped individuals to be free from discrimination against the legitimate concerns of exposing others to significant health risks.

In establishing the standard of "otherwise qualified," the Court developed a test based on four factors proposed by the American Medical Association in an amicus brief filed with the court. In utilizing the AMA's recommendations, the Court stated that findings of fact relative to the status of being "otherwise qualified" were to be made based on a "reasonable medical judgment" of:

- the nature of the risk (how the disease is transmitted)
- the duration of the risk (how long the carrier is infectious)
- the severity of the risk (the potential harm to third parties)
- the probabilities of transmission and cause of harm.

Incorporated within its decision in Arline, the Supreme Court maintained that even if an individual with a contagious disease is "handicapped," he or she is not "otherwise qualified" for an employment benefit or position if 1)he or she posed a significant risk of communicating an infectious disease to others in the workplace and 2)reasonable accommodation can not eliminate such a risk. The Court here implied that a case-by-case approach would be necessary to answer the question of whether a carrier of a contagious disease would be protected under the Vocational Rehabilitation Act. Determinations of coverage under the Act would involve an assessment by the Court of the nature of the disease relative to the above American Medical Association guidelines and a determination of the extent to which a specific employer should be required to accommodate the worker.

Several months after the Arline decision the federal district court for the District of Columbia applied the Arline court's interpretation of this standard of "otherwise qualified" in the case of Local 1812, American Federation of Government Employees v. United States Department of State. The court held that although foreign service employees who were HIV-infected were handicapped within the meaning of Section 504 of the Rehabilitation Act, they were not otherwise qualified for worldwide duty. The court based its conclusion on the fact that HIV-infected persons would be subject to poor medical care and unsanitary conditions in many posts and that these conditions would be harmful to impaired immune systems. Hence, while the Supreme Court's definition of otherwise qualified as presented in Arline appeared designed to protect otherwise healthy employees from HIV-infected coworkers, the decision in Local 1812 interpreted the definition from an altruistic concern for the infected employee's well-being. While this might appear to be a narrow interpretation and ruling, it was important in setting a precedent for altruistic concern as a means of justifying differential treatment of those infected with HIV. Hence, the decision appeared to provide employers with a potential justification or defense in discriminating against an HIV-infected employee.

Are Individuals with HIV-Infection Handicapped?

While the Supreme Court's decision in Arline clearly satisfied the question of whether contagious/communicable diseases are protected under Section 504 of the Rehabilitation Act, the question remained as to whether those with HIV are handicapped under Section 504. Clearly, individuals manifesting physical symptoms of full-blown AIDS will qualify under the first category of the Act's definition of a "handicapped individual," "a physical or mental impairment substantially limiting one or more major life activities." Persons with full-blown AIDS generally reach a point of being unable to care for themselves. Caring for oneself is one of the categories of "major life activities" as defined by the previously-cited Department of Health and Human Services guidelines. Nonetheless, this question was not answered in a federal court until 1988 when a ninth circuit appellate court issued a precedent-setting ruling.

In what has been the landmark case to date concerning the protection offered by Section 504 of the Rehabilitation Act to those with AIDS, a federal appeals court for the state of California reversed a lower court decision in Chalk v. United States District Court, Central District of California. In this case an instructor of hearing-impaired students was removed from his classroom duties and assigned to an administrative position with the same salary and benefits following his diagnosis of AIDS. Chalk filed suit under Section 504, requesting an injunction that would permit him to return to the classroom. While the district court denied his petition, the Ninth Circuit Court of Appeals reversed the decision, allowing the injunction. The court found that Chalk's "duties in the classroom present no significant risk to others and...although handicapped, because of AIDS, [Chalk] is otherwise qualified to perform his job within the meaning of Section 504 of the Rehabilitation Act." As a result, the district court was ordered to grant Chalk's motion for an injunction which returned him to his classroom position and former employment status while he waited for a full trial on the discrimination charges. This precedent of allowing a temporary injunction while the suit was pending later became a critical component of the outcome of the case.

As the Chalk verdict determined, the crucial question with respect to the statutory protection of all groups of HIV-infected persons under Section 504 is whether a given individual is "otherwise qualified" for employment. Following the reasoning presented in the Chalk case, even the mere "transfer" of a person with AIDS to another position comparable in salary is probably not an acceptable course of action by an employer unless there is a significant health risk to others such as holding a position involving invasive medical procedures. Otherwise, the HIV-infected individual remains "otherwise qualified" for his or her job and is therefore protected from any adverse employment action until he or she becomes physically or mentally unable to do his or her job. However, for those individuals with more advanced stages of AIDS, it may be plausible that a court might uphold discrimination or termination of employment. For example, when an individual with AIDS can not maintain an acceptable attendance record because of his or her condition, a court might conclude that such an individual is unable to perform the duties of the job, making him or her not otherwise qualified.

A provocative aspect of the Chalk case concerns the means by which both the district and appellate courts reached their conclusions. The district court relied heavily upon the second and third guidelines of the "otherwise qualified" rule established in the Arline case, citing the duration of the risk and severity of the risk. The appellate court, on the other hand, de-emphasized these factors in its reversal, giving greater weight to the first and fourth medical factors presented in the Arline decision, namely the nature of the risk and the probability of transmission. While the appellate ruling certainly overrides that of the lower court, the implication here is that interpretation of "otherwise qualified" is still somewhat ambiguous. The fact that courts can go either way in using Arline to justify their decisions implies that the status of future discrimination claims in this regard may not necessarily be that clear-cut. This could be particularly true in a case which was based on state employment anti-discrimination laws that utilize definitions not identical to those used in the Rehabilitation Act involving a private sector employment relationship. Nonetheless, Chalk was the first case in which a federal appeals court interpreted the Rehabilitation Act to include those with AIDS within its definition of protected handicapped workers.

Another particularly interesting aspect of the Chalk case concerns its handling of irreparable injury. Chalk was placed in an administrative job where he prepared grant proposals, at the same rate of pay and benefits he received when teaching. Chalk successfully argued that the alternative assignment substantially injured him even though he was not affected financially. The court concurred with Chalk's argument that the deprivation of use of his teaching skills and active contact with students constituted an injury. Such an argument was unprecedented in handicapped employment discrimination cases. This argument sends a strong warning that employers may not freely reassign a qualified employee with AIDS and can not rely on the absence of any monetary injury as a defense to the reassignment or transfer.

The Chalk decision clearly answered the question of whether individuals falling into type IV classification, those with full-blown AIDS who are still capable of working, qualify for protection under the Rehabilitation Act. The question still remained for courts to determine the same issue for those in classification types I, high risk group members, II, asymptomatic carriers of the virus, and III, those with mild symptoms of the disease or ARC. Regarding the first group, individuals discriminated against because they are perceived to have the virus could be covered under the third category of the statute's definition of a handicapped individual, defined as "individuals regarded as having such an impairment." Individuals with ARC may qualify as having a condition that "substantially limits one or more major life activities."

These classifications, however, may change. The federal government is currently eliminating the ARC category and combining it with those who suffer the full-blown effects and symptoms of AIDS. Public health officials are demanding this change by arguing that individuals with mild symptoms would qualify for experimental health care treatments that they are not now currently eligible to receive. Those advocating this position base their stance on the belief that earlier identification and treatment may slow the progression of full-blown AIDS. Despite the possible public health benefits of this proposed reclassification, the elimination of a clear distinct category of HIV infection might complicate the process of deciding employment discrimination claims. This is due to the vast differences in the ways the virus affects individuals. Those deciding cases might more easily evaluate facts if cases could be paralleled to a similar previously heard case, allowing comparisons of facts and issues. This would give a judge unfamiliar with HIV-based employment discrimination cases some basic guidelines.

While the Chalk case established that those with full-blown AIDS are protected under the Rehabilitation Act, it remained less obvious whether asymptomatic carriers of the virus would receive the same protection. Public health officials have argued that because the risk of contagion in the clear majority of job situations is negligible and avoidable, fear of transmissibility of HIV, particularly asymptomatic HIV, should not render an individual unqualified. The notion that asymptomatic individuals with contagious diseases would be considered handicapped under the Rehabilitation Act received some initial support in the case of Kohl by Kohl v. Woodhaven Learning Center. In this case, a federal district court for Western Missouri held in 1987 that asymptomatic infection with hepatitis B, a contagious virus, was a handicap under the Rehabilitation Act. In two additional cases, the courts have suggested that asymptomatic HIV infection is an impairment. This view supports the view that asymptomatics are protected by Section 504.

In the 1987 case of Thomas v. Atascadero Unified School District, the federal court for the central district of California stated that *those **infected** with the AIDS virus suffer significant impairment in their life activities...and may have difficulties caring for themselves, performing manual tasks, walking, seeing, hearing, speaking, breathing, learning and working, among other functions. Even those who are asymptomatic have abnormalities in their hemic and reproductive systems making procreation and childbirth dangerous to themselves and others.*

Childbirth, in this case, was considered to be a "major life activity" unlike in the North Carolina case of Burgess v. Your House of Raleigh where the court found that the abilities to bear a healthy child and engage in sexual relations were not "major life activities."

In the previously cited Local 1812, American Federation of Government Employees v. United States Department of State, a federal district court for the District of Columbia agreed with the State Department that "the great majority of HIV carriers are physically impaired and handicapped...due to measurable deficiencies in their immune systems even where disease symptoms have not yet developed."

Some additional arguments support these interpretations of Section 504. When Congress amended the Rehabilitation Act in 1982, it recognized that the unjustified concerns of others were among the chief obstacles faced by individuals with handicaps. Protecting asymptomatic HIV carriers would clearly advance support of this definition since these carriers are limited chiefly by the attitudes of others toward their condition. Also, it may be contested that the third category of the Rehabilitation Act's definition of a handicapped person protects asymptomatic carriers as well as those mistakenly perceived as infected with AIDS because they are *viewed* as having an impairment, hence satisfying the statute's requirements. Asymptomatic HIV infection can limit an individual's ability to work because of the reluctance of employers to hire, and others to work with, that individual.

Medical experts concur that the mere presence of the virus results in a heightened risk of future symptomatic illness, illness that would manifest itself if the virus becomes active. Even when the virus is not active, a carrier can exhibit several asymptomatic, but diagnosable, abnormal immune functions that indicate an impaired ability to fight infection. Hence, the afflicted person has an increased risk of future symptomatic disability. While all of this may imply that asymptomatic infection constitutes a handicap, it should be remembered that in order for a handicapped individual to be protected from discrimination under the Act, such asymptomatic infection must also be shown to substantially limit a major life activity.

Civil Rights Restoration Act

The classification of HIV infection as a protected handicap under Section 504 became a bit less vague when, in 1988, Congress overrode the veto of President Reagan and passed the Civil Rights Restoration Act of 1987. This act promoted the classification of HIV-infected persons as handicapped individuals" under Section 504 and amended the definition of "handicapped individual" in the Rehabilitation Act so as to codify the legal precedent set in the Supreme Court's Arline decision. The amendment indicated that the main issue to be addressed in whether those with communicable disease were covered under Section 504 was the extent to which infected individuals were "otherwise qualified." This involved an assessment of the risk of communicability, and the extent to which the employer could "reasonably accommodate" the employee.

More specifically, the Civil Rights Restoration Act amended Section 706 (8) of the Rehabilitation Act by adding the following new section after subparagraph (b):

(c) For the purpose of Sections 503 and 504, as such sections relate to employment, such erm does not include an individual who has a currently contagious disease or infection and who, by reason of such disease or infection, would constitute a direct threat to the health or safety of other individuals or who, by reason of the currently contagious disease or infection, is unable to perform the duties of the job.

This amendment, named after its sponsors, Senators Tom Harkin and Gordon Humphrey, is controversial due to the fact that its sponsors disagree as to its precise meaning. Senator Harkin stated that the amendment is consistent with and codifies Arline. It protects those with contagious diseases against job discrimination if they are qualified to do the job and present no threat to coworkers. Senator Humphrey stated that the intent of the amendment is to assure employers that they are not required to retain or hire individuals with contagious or infectious diseases when an inability to perform or health threat concerns exist. While Harkin sponsored the amendment as a means of preserving and extending the right of handicapped employees, Humphrey promoted it in advocacy of supporting employers who can legally justify a reason to discriminate.

It is interesting that the Supreme Court's Arline decision, which specifically stated that it was not a ruling as to whether those with HIV were covered under the Rehabilitation Act, became the foundation for an amendment that was very broad and vague. While it could be interpreted to include those with HIV, it lacked so much in specifics that one sponsor saw it as protection for workers against handicapped discrimination while its other sponsor saw it as an employer defense against such charges. Although the Civil Rights Restoration Act amendment has yet to be fully interpreted by the courts, it appears to obviate the distinction between the actual disabling effects and perceived threats raised in the 1986 Department of Justice memorandum. It implies that when infectious diseases are the basis for a handicap discrimination claim, only the actual threat to others posed by the presence of the individual in the workplace and the individual's ability to perform the job in question are relevant.

The amendment was put to the test later in 1988 when the federal court for the central district of California heard the case Doe v. Centinela Hospital. The court ruled that excluding a person from a rehabilitation program in a federally funded hospital because he tested positive for the HIV virus was an exclusion of an "individual with handicaps" within the meaning of the Rehabilitation Act's Section 504. In relying on the fact that the likelihood of transmission of HIV to others was extremely minimal, the court addressed the issue of whether asymptomatic individuals, and possibly even those with mild symptoms or ARC, were handicapped and covered under Section 504.

Revised Opinion of the Department of Justice

In direct response to this legislative and judicial activity which now included HIV coverage under the Rehabilitation Act, on September 27, 1988 the United States Department of Justice revised its earlier opinion and reversed its previous decision. In doing so it publicly endorsed the expansion of the Rehabilitation Act's protection to both asymptomatic and symptomatic carriers of the HIV virus. It based its position on the opinion that these individuals were handicapped within the context of an employment setting to the extent that no risk was posed to coworkers and the individual was not prevented from performing his or her job responsibilities. While this appeared to be a significant announcement, this Department of Justice decision would probably not altogether eliminate discrimination against HIV-infected individuals. Discrimination might easily continue if the individual is found to not be "substantially limited" in major life activities unless the courts find that HIV infection manifestations in and of themselves represent a substantial impairment. In other words, the Rehabilitation Act requires that an individual be "substantially limited in one of more major life activities" to be protected. If any court reasoned that asymptomatic HIV infection did not limit any major life activities, it could rule that asymptomatic infection was not protected.

Limitations of the Rehabilitation Act

While at this juncture it may appear that HIV status is increasingly being seen as a protected handicap under the Rehabilitation Act, it is critical to remember the Act's limited coverage. In covering only the actions of the federal government, its contractors and subcontractors, and recipients of its funds and grants, the vast majority of Americans remain unprotected by the Act unless covered by either a collective bargaining agreement that specifically addresses the issue of handicaps or relevant state or municipal laws. While all fifty states and the District of Columbia prohibit employment discrimination against the handicapped, the treatment of the subject by each state varies quite extensively. Georgia and Kentucky, for example, specifically exclude "communicable diseases" from their coverage and New Hampshire excludes coverage for disability "by virtue of illness." A number of states do define a "handicapped person" using the same criteria of three classifications. However, the variety of definitions and inclusions/exclusions still leaves many workers unprotected from discrimination, particularly if employed by a private sector employer. It must be remembered that the Rehabilitation Act was passed in 1973 and many state laws predicated on this Act were hence codified prior to the discovery of the HIV virus and the illness AIDS. Hence, they are unable to address the condition directly as such a handicapping condition could not have been anticipated by legislators or society at the time of promulgation.

Americans with Disabilities Act

In 1990, realizing that existing handicapped discrimination statutes were probably insufficient, Congress passed the Americans With Disabilities Act. Proponents of the Act reproached the Rehabilitation Act's limited scope and noted that the new bill was intended to protect the many individuals in private and public employment left unprotected against discrimination by then-current disability legislation. The Act extended the coverage of the Vocational Rehabilitation Act to all employers with fifteen or more employees with its scope of coverage identical to that of the Civil Rights Act of 1964. Specifically it extends the Rehabilitation Act to "any employer, employment agency, labor organization or joint labor-management committee with fifteen of more employees" and prohibits discrimination against "any qualified individual with a disability because of such disability in regard to job application procedures, hiring or discharge of employees, employee compensation, advancement, job training and other terms, conditions, and practice of employment." The Act went into effect on January 26, 1992 for employers with 25 or more employees and provided an extended two-year grace period for employers with 15-24 employees.

While it provides the same remedies for discrimination as Civil Rights Act, the Disabilities Act's language retains most of the Rehabilitation Act's definitions and essentially requires covered employers to follow the terms of the Rehabilitation Act. Under the Americans With Disabilities Act, a disability is defined as "a physical or mental impairment that substantially limits one or more of the major life activities of such individual," "a record of such impairment," or "being regarded as having such an impairment" which is exactly the same terminology employed in the Rehabilitation Act.

Despite its similarities to the Rehabilitation Act and other laws, the Americans With Disabilities Act breaks new ground on several fronts. The first of these involves an enumeration of eight specific types of conduct which would constitute employment discrimination. Title I, Section 102 (b) of the Act defines discrimination to include:

1. adversely classifying an applicant or employee because of his or her disability;

2. participating in a contractual relationship that has the effect of discriminating against qualified applicants or employees with disabilities;

3. using standards or procedures which have the effect of discrimination on the basis of disability or which perpetuate such effect;

4. denying qualified individuals equal jobs or benefits because they associate with an individual known to have a disability;

5. not making reasonable accommodations to the known physical or mental limitations of a qualified individual who is an applicant or employee, unless such covered entity can demonstrate that the accommodation would impose an undue hardship on the operation of the business or such covered entity;

6. denying employment opportunities to a job applicant or employee who is a qualified individual with a disability, if such denial is based on the need of such covered entity to make reasonable accommodation to the physical or mental impairment of the employee or applicant;

7. using employment tests or other selection criteria which have a disparate impact on individuals with disabilities unless the test or selection criteria can be shown to be job-related and consistent with business necessity;

8. failing to administer employment tests in a manner which most accurately reflects the job related skills of employees and applicants with disabilities.

Another distinguishing aspect of the Act is that under the above sub-sections 5 and 6, it requires employers to make "reasonable accommodations" to the known physical or mental limitations of qualified individuals unless those accommodations "would impose an undue hardship on the operation of the business." While the Rehabilitation Act does require "reasonable accommodation," it doesn't define any such accommodations in specific terms. The ADA, however, does so in Section 101(9) and includes, under reasonable accommodation, "making existing facilities usable by individuals with disabilities" as well as "job restructuring, part-time or modified work schedules, reassignment to a vacant position, acquisition or modification of equipment or devices, appropriate adjustment or modifications of examinations, training materials, or policies...and other similar accommodations for individuals with disabilities."

Such reasonable accommodation can be denied if, under section 102 (b)(5), if it creates an "undue hardship" upon the employer. The only guidance the Act provides in assessing the state of an accommodation as an undue hardship is provided in Section 101 (9)(A) of the Act which defines such a hardship as "an action requiring significant difficulty or expense." Like the Rehabilitation Act, the Americans With Disabilities Act lists general factors to be considered in assessing whether a particular accommodation would create an undue hardship. Some of these factors are the overall size of the employer's business, its type of operation, and the nature and cost of the accommodation. The intent of Congress here implies that a case-by-case analysis must be made concerning "undue hardship." While the statute is vague and offers no specific guidelines, the standard would clearly be determined relative to the physical and financial resources of the employer. Hence, what might be reasonable for a large resource-abundant employer, could constitute an undue hardship for a smaller employer. Nonetheless, the vagueness of the statute in this regard could easily be a point of contention in an alleged discrimination charge.

The ADA also departs from the Rehabilitation Act in that the former allows, in Section 103(a), "qualification standards" or criteria that are "job-related and consistent with business necessity, where such performance cannot be accomplished by reasonable accommodation." In other words, requirements related to the performance of specific tasks may be established that are not intentionally designed to exclude specific categories of workers. Further, under Section 103(b), this "qualification standard" may require that an individual not "pose a direct threat to the health and safety of other individuals in the workplace". For most workers, however, this "qualification standard" should not be an issue, given the near-zero probability of casual workplace transmission. However, in the cases of health care and law enforcement and corrections workers, the significance of any threat being posed by an HIV-infected individual that a worker comes in contact with within the course of his or her job responsibilities remains under debate.

Summary

Despite all of the above facts and analysis, the question still remains concerning the extent to which individuals who have been exposed to or believed to be at high risk for contracting the HIV virus are protected under federal handicapped employment discrimination law. Uniform consensus has not been established among the courts for a number of reasons. Vague statutory terms such as "otherwise qualified" and "reasonable accommodation," among others, further illustrate that there are no hard set standards for an employer concerning employment of the handicapped. Further, the fact that HIV infection has multiple manifestations makes the disease a non-standard ailment. Hence, a precedent established in one case might not be cited in another case. Similarly, the different classifications of HIV infection might require different "tests" and "rules" for courts to use relative to these different classifications.

Under current handicap discrimination law, those with full-blown AIDS who retain the capacity to work would probably have the best chance of statutory protection under the first definition of "handicapped individual" under the Rehabilitation and Americans with Disabilities Acts; that is "an actual physical or mental impairment which substantially limits one or more major life activities." Those diagnosed with ARC or with milder symptoms of the disease, would probably find that their protection depends on the current state of infection and the extent to which it "substantially limits" them. Otherwise, with no impairment, they might find the best protection under the third definition of handicapped, "regarded as having a physical or mental impairment."

Asymptomatic individuals infected with HIV might find protection under any of the three classifications: the first classification of handicapped if exposure to the virus itself is interpreted to constitute an "impairment"; under the second classification, "having a record of impairment," if the individual previously exhibited symptoms but is currently in remission; or under the third classification if no physical or mental impairment can be proven. Individuals who are members of high-risk groups for transmission of the virus might find protection under the third definition of handicapped, "regarded as having an impairment," but only to the extent that their membership in a high-risk group was known by the employer. Under any such claims utilizing the third definition, "regarded as having an impairment," the employee only needs to establish that the employer treated the employee as having an impairment that substantially limits major life activities; the employee need not be required to establish an actual impairment.

The current state of the "art" of proving that the HIV virus represents a handicapped condition under federal employment discrimination law, is not fully developed and fraught with questions and uncertainty. While certain landmark cases cited above can support inclusion of HIV for protection under the statutes, the language used in both the statutes and decisions leaves a good deal of legal leeway for such claims to be open to interpretation of the specific case facts. Further, given that HIV infection and AIDS as a disease tend to be dramatically different from other types of disabilities routinely encountered in the workplace implies that decisions relative to other disabilities may be of little guiding precedence in cases involving HIV. To date no Supreme Court case has been heard that specifically concerns HIV as a handicapping condition relative to employment. Hence there exists no set parameters nor a framework for interpretation of the statutes. Consequently, given projected increases in HIV-related illness and accompanying discrimination, it is likely that many more cases will be presented to lower courts. These courts will need to continue to interpret the existing body of law to determine the true intentions of legislatures before a case reaches the Supreme Court. Hence, a systematic framework for understanding the applicability of handicap discrimination statutes to HIV infection and for evaluating any such future claims has yet to be developed.

3

Protection in Different Stages of HIV Infection

This chapter provides an analysis of all reported discrimination cases based on HIV status since the beginning of the epidemic. Presented is an examination of each of the four classifications of HIV infection where individuals maintain the ability to work. These analyses first examine cases decided for the plaintiff to determine the legal principles on which these decisions were based and the definitions assigned to ambiguous statutory terms, such as "reasonable accomodation" and "otherwise qualified." The same process is repeated for cases in which judgment was issued for the defendant employer. Each of the four sections concludes with a brief discussion that develops the legal issues and principles into a framework for that particular classification of HIV infection.

Cases Involving High-Risk Group Members

The third category of the Vocational Rehabilitation Act defines a handicapped person as one who suffers discrimination because of the perceptions and attitudes of others. As previously discussed, this leaves much room for individual interpretation as to the inclusion of specific individuals or classes of individuals. While the number of cases decided relative to this classification is not large, the cases nonetheless illustrate some interesting trends.

Judgments for the Plaintiff

The case of Estate of McKinley v. Boston Harbor Hotel involved an openly gay plaintiff who worked as a dining room waiter. McKinley was hired in August, 1987 and subsequently diagnosed with HIV infection but showed no signs of symptoms until 1990 and *never informed* his employer of his health status. Throughout this time, he received consistent performance evaluations of "excellent" and "outstanding." When he returned to work after taking three weeks medical leave due to a resparitory ailment in May and June, 1990, McKinley was repeatedly assigned the least desirable stations. He serviced fewer tables than other waitpersons and his superiors constantly scrutinized his work closely. In addition managers repeatedly asked co-workers if they knew whether McKinley had AIDS. McKinley resigned in July, 1990 due to the harassment but still maintained that he could perform his job responsibilities effectively.

The plaintiff filed a complaint based on his perceived handicap with the Massachusetts Commission Against Discrimination. The defendants argued that since McKinley *never told management about his condition*, he was not protected by the statute. The Commission found that the employer violated the Massachusetts Fair Employment Act by reaching "the inescapable conclusion that the employer did indeed perceive McKinley to have AIDS," and that those perceived to have AIDS were covered under the statute, regardless of the presence or absence of symptoms. Key evidence cited here was the testimony of McKinley's former co-workers regarding the questions asked by management concerning McKinley's health. This case, decided in 1992, was the first case to receive a hearing in Massachusetts relative to the issue of perceived disability. It conveyed the message that employers can not feign ignorance when "obvious signs" of disability are present. The estate of the deceased plaintiff was awarded $30,000 in compensatory damages and legal fees, ordered to cease discriminating against people with AIDS, and to institute an AIDS education program for supervisors.

In another case from New England heard before a state commission, a travel agency fired an employee following the death of his lover from an AIDS-related illness. In Connecticut Human Rights Commission v. Respondent, the employer perceived the employee to be carrying the HIV virus and fired him for that reason. The Commission found the employer in violation of state law because the state anti-discrimination statute prohibits discrimination of individuals who are physically disabled or perceived to be physically disabled. In finding HIV infection to be a physical disability and hence within the protection offered by law, the commission awarded the employee monetary damages and ordered the employer to educate its employees concerning the need for nondiscriminatory conduct towards those infected with HIV.

In the case of Sanchez v. Lagoudakis, Sanchez was employed as a waitress at Lagoudakis' restaurant. The defendant had been satisfied with her work until patrons complained that "she had AIDS." Based on these unsubstantiated rumors, the defendant told the plaintiff not to return to work until she could prove her HIV antibody status was negative. While the plaintiff paid for an HIV test and tested negative, she declined to return to work and filed a suit alleging discrimination under the Michigan Handicapper's Civil Rights Act.

The court held that the MHCRA did not extend protection to those with perceived, but not actual handicaps. Its reasoning involved the fact that unlike the Vocational Rehabilitation Act, the Michigan statute's definition of a handicap did not expressly include perceived handicaps. The court declined to expand the MHCRA without evidence of legislative intent and declined to comment on public policy arguments made by the plaintiff and the Michigan Organization for Human Rights, which had submitted an amicus curiae (friend of the court) brief. The court reasoned that "such arguments are best made to, and decided by the legislature."

On appeal, the Michigan Supreme Court reversed the lower court's decision. The high court reasoned that the significant issue here was the employer's motivation rather than the employee's physical condition. Regardless of whether the employee was actually handicapped, "the employer has undertaken the kind of discriminatory action that the Act prohibits." It is noteworthy that since the case was originally decided in 1990, the MHCRA has been amended to expressly include perceived handicaps.

There was an additional case involving an individual belonging to a high-risk group. That person, an openly gay employee of an adult bookstore, was also perceived to be HIV-infected. In State of Minnesota v. Di Ma Corporation and Richard Carriveau, the commissioner of the state Department of Human Rights brought action on behalf of Lyle Pierce, the employee of Carriveau, the owner of the bookstore. Pierce, a sales clerk, was required in 1987 to be tested for HIV due to Carriveau's fears that the latter might "catch it himself" from his gay employee. Pierce tested positive but had the reported results altered to show a negative result. In 1988, Pierce was promoted to manager but during the fall of that year lost fifty pounds. Although Pierce argued that dieting caused the weight loss, Carriveau suspected AIDS and harassed Pierce on the job. In early 1989, Carriveau terminated Pierce for poor performance and offered him five weeks severance pay to resign and avoid unemployment hearings. Carriveau reconsidered the terms and then offered to retain Pierce if the latter signed an undated open-ended letter of resignation. Carriveau later pressured Pierce to be retested and when Pierce refused he was "fired" in accordance with the terms of the letter he had signed.

The Minnesota Department of Human Rights found that Pierce was discriminated against due to his disability. Even though Carriveau didn't know Pierce's HIV status, the latter was treated discriminatorily because his employer perceived him to be carrying the HIV virus. The department further ruled that HIV-positive status is a physical impairment that limits a major life activity, hence constituting disability. Further, the defendant did not prove that absence of HIV infection is a bona fide occupational qualification for the position of manager of his bookstore. The administrative law judge required reinstatement and back pay plus interest and punitive damages totalling $44,749 as well as payment of a civil fine of $25,000.

Judgments for the Defendant

Despite these cases in which the plaintiffs have received protection against discrimination resulting from the perceptions of others that they are HIV-infected, several cases have been judged in the defendant's favor. In Petri v. Bank of New York Co. Inc. a judge found the defendant did not violate the New York Human Rights Act. The plaintiff was allegedly fired for insubordination but claimed his termination was due to discrimination of his employer's perception of his having AIDS and/or his membership in a high-risk group for contracting the virus. The plaintiff presented evidence of the defendant's knowledge of his prior sexual relationship with an HIV-positive man and further argued that his termination was an attempt by his employer to save money in the event that he did eventually develop AIDS.

The court found no violation of the Act as the plaintiff was considered an at-will employee. While stating that those who have tested positive for HIV are handicapped under the Act, it found that the plaintiff did not have HIV nor did he test positive to constitute perceived disability. While the plaintiff was known to be gay, the court found that "mere membership in a high-risk group being equivalent to a perceived disability would be to impart into the statute a ban on sexual orientation discrimination that the legislature has specifically failed to pass." Further, it found that there was no evidence to substantiate the claim that the motivating force in the dismissal was proof of an illness or a perception of an illness. The key issue here was that the plaintiff did not claim to be afflicted with a disease, either seropositivity for HIV or full-blown AIDS. Hence, under this ruling someone who has been exposed to HIV infection but has not come down with physical symptoms has not established a disability for which a recovery in damages may be allowed.

In the case of Rose City Oil v. Missouri Commission on Human Rights, the plaintiff employer appealed an earlier decision by the Commission relative to its alleged violation of the Missouri Human Rights Act. Rose City Oil was the parent company of the Cut-Rite convenience store chain. In 1987, managers at a Benton, Missouri Cut-Rite store learned from a customer that an employee, Scott McClanahan, was rumored to be HIV-positive. Management immediately reassigned McClanahan from his responsibilities as a sandwich maker to cashier. Later fired for alleged insubordination, McClanahan filed a claim with the Commission alleging discrimination based on handicap, in this case a perceived handicap. As with many other such state statutes the Missouri

Act had adopted the Rehabilitation Act's definition of a handicap (including "perceived" cases).

The court answered the question of whether the mere perception of HIV infection was enough to sustain a claim under the MHRA even if the individual was treated in an apparently discriminatory manner in favor of the employer. It found that the claim did not establish that a handicap existed within the statute despite the express inclusion of those perceived to be handicapped. The court interpreted the state's definition of handicapped to exclude those perceived as being handicapped who didn't actually have handicaps. It found that any perception of a handicap required the "*existence of a condition* which might be perceived as a handicap." In other words, perceptions, in and of themselves, were not actionable unless the accompanying condition actually existed as well. This case, decided in 1992, represented the first time a court had required a handicap to exist in order for perceptions concerning it to be actionable.

In addition to this, the court further found that McClanahan had not been discriminated against in his reassignment to cashier. The rationale for this was the fact that McClanahan's job description included both sandwich making and cashier duties and exclusive assignment or reassignment to one area was allowed, particularly in the light that the reassignment in this instance involved neither a pay cut nor any substantive change in working conditions.

An additional case relating to an individual perceived to be infected with HIV was heard at both the federal and state level. The federal suit was based on the fact that the Louisiana hospital district being sued received federal funding. In Leckelt v. Board of Commissioners of Hospital District No. 1, the plaintiff worked as an LPN in a hospital. His job duties including changing patient's dressings, giving medication both orally and by injection, starting intravenous lines, performing catherizations and administering enemas. The hospital staff knew that the plaintiff was gay and that his roommate of eight years, who had been a patient of the hospital, had recently died from an AIDS-related condition. The hospital also knew that the plaintiff was a Hepatitis B virus carrier and had previously been infected with syphilis. The hospital had also diagnosed the plaintiff with general lymphadenopathy, a condition indicative of recent HIV infection. The hospital requested HIV test results from the plaintiff who refused to comply and subsequently fired him for violating hospital disease control policy which required all employees to report any "infectious or communicable diseases" with which they were afflicted.

The federal court found that the hospital was not in violation of the Vocational Rehabilitation Act in its alleged discrimination of Leckelt on the basis of a perceived handicap. It found that the defendant was dismissed for failure to comply with hospital policies, not because he was perceived to be HIV-infected. The court further found that although there was strong indication of HIV infection, Leckelt was fired for not obeying hospital infection control policy by submitting to the testing.

The court further found that the plaintiff was not "otherwise qualified" for his job notwithstanding his perceived handicap. Because some of Leckelt's duties involved invasive procedures and because he failed to comply with hospital policy concerning infectious diseases, he was not otherwise qualified to perform his job as a nurse. In addition, by failing to report his HIV status to hospital officials, Leckelt prevented the hospital from knowing whether he actually had a handicap that required accommodation.

A similar decision was reached at the state level. The hospital was found to be in compliance with the Louisiana Civil Rights of Handicapped Persons Act. In its reasoning the court found that the Act was inapplicable to the case because it would require discrimination based on the results of an HIV test and as Leckelt had failed to submit any test results, there was no basis for a claim as Leckelt had not established the fact that he was indeed handicapped.

Discussion

While the body of case law is not substantial in terms of volume, it is significant in helping to draw a conclusion as to whether those perceived to be infected with HIV or be at risk for it are protected under the law. Courts in different states have interpreted their own state laws differently, despite the fact that their definition of what constitutes a handicap has been adapted from the Vocational Rehabilitation Act.

In those cases decided for the defendant, a critical factor in the verdict appears to be whether or not the employee who was allegedly discriminated against had tested positive for HIV. In all of the cases decided in the employer's favor, a key piece of evidence was that the plaintiff employees had not provided positive test results. However, in all of the cases decided in the employee's favor, positive test results were considered insignificant to the verdict.

The Americans With Disabilities Act, which now supplements existing state laws, utilizes the Rehabilitation Act's definition of a handicap in its own definition of a disability as does many of the individual state statutes. Hence, it is still unclear the extent to which those perceived to be at risk for HIV or perceived to be infected with HIV can find protection against discrimination in employment.

Leckelt v. Board of Commissioners of Hospital District No. 1, the only case that has been heard under federal law (the Rehabilitation Act), was decided in favor of the defendant employer but also had the unique facts of a plaintiff who was of highly questionable health working in a health care environment. Therefore, Leckelt may be interpreted by other courts within these parameters and not be seen as legal precedent. However, the significant ruling in the case involves the fact that Leckelt's protection under the law was predecessed on his testing positive. This implies that those who are merely perceived as being HIV-infected may find no protection from employment discrimination absent positive proof through test results.

Cases Involving HIV-Positive Asymptomatic Individuals

Surprisingly, the greatest number of cases of employment discrimination were against those who had tested HIV-positive without exhibiting any symptoms of the disease. The manner in which the courts have handled these cases has had significant variation as discussed below.

Judgments for the Plaintiff

In the 1990 case of Benjamin R. v. Orkin Exterminating Co., Inc. the state court ruled that under the West Virginia Human Rights Act, an HIV-positive person is handicapped within the meaning of the Act. The plaintiff in this case worked as a pest control inspector for the defendant company. He tested positive for HIV in January, 1987 and informed his supervisor of this six months later. One month after informing his supervisor of his HIV status, the plaintiff was fired and informed that the termination was due to his seropositivity. He filed a complaint with the West Virginia Human Rights Commission which certified his suit in state court for alleged employment discrimination based on handicap

The court ruled that regardless of the stage of HIV infection, the state statute had two requirements that must be met for a handicap; a physical or mental impairment and evidence that the impairment "substantially limited one or more major life activities." The court found that even in its earliest stages, HIV infection involves a physical impairment of the body's blood and immune systems. It further found the major life activity of socialization to be substantially limited by HIV infection as "almost all HIV patients are withdrawn, depressed or suicidal." It is noteworthy that the court found unpersuasive a decision cited by the defense that was issued in the North Carolina case Burgess v. Your House of Raleigh which stated that the ability to bear a healthy child and engage in sexual relations were not "major life activities."

The court also found a public policy reason to include HIV infection within the definition of a handicap. It reasoned that by preventing employment discrimination, early testing and disclosure would be encouraged, enabling those who must take precautions to do so; the court reasoned that "from a public health standpoint, it is critical for all people at all stages of HIV infection to be assured of legal protection from unlawful discrimination."

An earlier West Virginia case heard under the same act reached a similar conclusion via a different rationale. In Isbell v. Poor Richard's, the plaintiff, a waiter, was fired and claimed that the action was due to his HIV seropositivity which amounted to illegal discrimination under the West Virginia Human Rights Act. The defendant argued that the firing was due to sloppy work habits but immediately after the firing also attempted to have the restaurant declared a private club, making it beyond the jurisdiction of the human rights regulations. The court found that the restaurant's actions amounted to illegal discrimination under the Act on the basis of a *perceived* handicap.

In its decision, the court ordered the defendant to pay the plaintiff $38,500 for legal fees and expenses, $2,000 for humiliation and emotional distress, $6,300 for back wages and to reinstate the plaintiff. Another significant fact of the case involved the court's finding that the employer could not rely on the defense of "customer preference" to justify otherwise unlawful discrimination. While the issue of alleged customer preference had previously arisen in several employment discrimination cases based on gender, this marked the first time that the defense was applied to HIV infection.

In the case of Buler v. Southland Corporation, d/b/a (doing business as) Seven-Eleven Stores, Inc., an argument similar to the one presented in Isbell resulted in a judgment for the plaintiff but the decision extended the rationale one step further. Buler, a sales and inventory clerk at a 7-11 store in Baltimore, was informed by his store manager, nine months after being hired, that his continued employment was contingent upon a negative HIV test. Upon receiving a positive result, Buler was repeatedly encouraged by his manager to commit suicide. The manager disclosed the results of Buler's test to his family, friends, and coworkers, and finally fired him. After being fired, Buler attempted to find similar work but was repeatedly rejected. He became depressed and suicidal and, after spending several weeks in a psychiatric hospital, became homeless.

The court found that the defendant unfairly discriminated against Buler based on the manager's *perception* that Buler suffered from AIDS, a recognized handicap under Maryland law. The court took the analysis one step further than the Isbell decision by stating that the plaintiff's condition was not a risk to coworkers and that he remained *otherwise qualified* to retain his position. Reinstatement was ordered with back wages and benefits along with a further order for the company to revise its employment policies to insure non-discriminatory treatment of those with handicaps.

In the case of Doe v. District of Columbia, the plaintiff was offered a position as a firefighter after passing written and physical examinations. When he informed the department of his HIV-positive status prior to reporting for the first day of work, he was informed that the offer had been revoked. Doe sued under the Vocational Rehabilitation Act.

The court found that Doe had been illegally denied employment solely due to his handicap. It stated that the applicant was *otherwise qualified* to perform the duties of a firefighter and posed *no measurable risk* of infecting either other firefighters or the public. The court concluded that the risk of Doe transmitting HIV to others in the line of duty could be compared "to that of being struck by a meteor" and that there were no reported cases of transmission by firefighting or emergency personnel through their job duties. Doe was awarded more than three years of back pay and $25,000 in compensatory damages for emotional distress. The court also issued an injunction forbidding the District from discriminating and denying employment based on HIV status.

The case of an HIV-infected employee who knowingly conceals his seropositivity was dealt with in Hummer v. Unemployment Appeals Commission. Hummer was employed as a full-time salesperson for a paging services company and, as a condition of employment, was entitled to ten paid sick days and two paid personal days per year. He informed his supervisor that he wished to take one of these days off each month to attend a manufacturer's meeting for a line of baby products he sold on the side. When the supervisor sought approval from the regional manager, the latter insisted on reimbursement for days already taken and forbade future days from being taken. Hummer disclosed his HIV seropositivity and informed management that the reason for his absence had been to receive medical treatment. Hummer was then given the option of resigning or having his employment terminated. When Hummer refused to resign, he was fired and was denied subsequent requests for unemployment compensation. The basis for the denial was that the former employer argued that Hummer was discharged because of his untruthfulness, which the Unemployment Appeals Commission affirmed in denying Hummer benefits. Hummer filed suit against the Commission.

The court found that Hummer's behavior did not constitute misconduct warranting the denial of benefits as defined by the unemployment compensation laws of Florida. It found Hummer to be an exemplary employee who exhibited no disloyalty or untruthfulness except regarding his medical condition. It acknowledged that the state legislature expressly recognized that people with AIDS suffer from irrational discrimination and found that the deception on Hummer's part appeared to be designed to protect his own privacy and not to harm his employer. It further found that the employer was not harmed by Hummer's actions.

The decision was found to be "at most an error in judgment and not a willful or intentional and substantial disregard of his employer's interests or of his duties."

It is interesting to note that Hummer did not file a suit against his employer for his termination despite the fact that Florida law includes HIV infection as a handicap. It is not known why Hummer did not file suit, nor did the court address the actions of the employer in its decision.

What constitutes "reasonable accommodation" of HIV-infected employees under federal law is addressed in Buckingham v. United States of America. The plaintiff began work in May, 1988 at the U.S. Post Office in Columbus, Mississippi. Having been diagnosed as HIV-positive in 1985, Buckingham requested reassignment in September, 1988 to Los Angeles in order to obtain better medical care. His request was denied due to a collective bargaining agreement whose terms stipulated that incumbents needed to have one year in their previous positions before being eligible for reassignment. The plaintiff filed suit under the Rehabilitation Act against the Los Angeles post office for failure to make reasonable accommodation for a handicapped employee.

The court concluded that the Rehabilitation Act had been violated by the Postal Service's failure to make reasonable accommodation for an employee with a handicap. It found that the postal service should not assert its one-year requirement in cases where the requirement clearly conflicts with its obligations under the Rehabilitation Act. This was based on the finding that the reassignment would not conflict with the rights of any other employees seeking transfer. The presiding judge ruled that this was "the very type of discrimination the Rehabilitation Act seeks to prevent." In finding that the plaintiff proposed a reasonable accommodation in seeking transfer to allow him to obtain medical treatment, the defendant rejected the proposal despite the lack of undue hardship on the employer and offered Buckingham no alternative accommodation. Buckingham was awarded the transfer with backpay, full seniority, fringe benefits and attorney's fees.

In Kautz v. Humana Hospital-Lucerne, another case dealing with reasonable accomodation, a hospital that failed to offer an HIV-positive surgical technician an alternative position was found to be in violation of the Rehabilitation Act. Kautz's job as a surgical technician involved assisting surgeons in holding open chest cavities, holding organs and providing surgeons with medical instruments. After learning that the plaintiff was HIV-positive, the hospital placed Kautz on suspension and wouldn't allow him to return to work at the hospital. The court found for the plaintiff in that, like Buckingham, the hospital didn't attempt to provide "reasonable accommodation" by providing Kautz with another position and further, did not provide him with the usual internal review procedures that precede termination of employment.

In another case involving a health care institution, a medical center was found to be in violation of both state and federal law in discriminating against an HIV-positive employee. In Doe v. Westchester County Medical Center, the plaintiff applied for and was offered a job as a pharmacist with the medical center. His medical records compiled as a patient at the institution indicated that he had previously tested positive for HIV. When this was discovered, the employment offer was withdrawn and the plaintiff subsequently filed suit against the medical center.

The court found that the medical center violated the New York State Human Rights Act by discriminating against an individual with a handicap and ordered the medical center to hire Doe *but* reminded the center to comply with state rules that limited the employment of pharmacists with infectious diseases. The court also awarded Doe $30,000 for mental anguish, humiliation and attorney's fees.

Doe also filed suit in federal court alleging employment discrimination based on handicap under the Vocational Rehabilitation Act. In this case the court found the hospital to be in violation of the Rehabilitation Act. Since the center had defied the lower court's order it also ordered the medical center to hire Doe. The court also awarded Doe back pay as well as transfer and seniority rights in addition to the lower courts award for mental anguish, humiliation and attorney's fees. The federal court then overturned the lower court's mandate by requiring that Doe be hired without restrictions on his job duties in accordance with the request of the Office of Civil Rights of the federal Department of Health and Human Services. While the court clearly found Doe to meet the definition of an individual with a handicap, it also found that "while there is a theoretical possibility of HIV transmission, the probability is so small as not to be measurable."

When the medical center refused to comply with this decision, the federal Department of Health and Human Services filed for and received a court order against the Westchester County Medical Center, requiring it to risk forfeiture of all of its federal funding (totalling $107 million annually) unless it hired Doe without placing restrictions on his duties. This landmark case represented the first civil rights enforcement action based on HIV discrimination filed by any federal agency. It set a major precedent for action against employers who receive federal funds or contracts.

Judgments for the Defendant

While asymptomatic HIV-positive employees have received significantly favorable treatment by the courts, several other plaintiffs have found their rights relative to employment discrimination to be less well defined. In fact, several of the aforementioned cases decided in favor of the plaintiff can be contrasted to cases with similar facts that were decided in favor of the defendant.

In the case of Burgess v. Your House of Raleigh, Inc., asymptomatic HIV infection was found to be an unprotected handicap under the North Carolina Handicapped Persons Protection Act. Burgess was employed as a short-order cook at the defendant's restaurant. When the owner learned of the plaintiff's HIV seropositivity, the defendant was immediately fired. Both parties freely admitted that the firing was based solely on HIV status. The plaintiff sued under the state act and the trial court found for the defendant that HIV seropositivity was not a protected handicap under the Act.

Upon appeal, the appellate court affirmed the decision of the lower court. It found HIV-infection to be expressly excluded from the state Act because it was a communicable disease and the Act contained an express exclusion of people with communicable diseases in its definition of what constitutes a handicap. It found the plaintiff's claim of HIV being a protected handicap to be "absurd." The court also ruled that to be handicapped within the meaning of the Act, one or more "major life activities" must be impaired and that HIV-positive status alone did not impair, finding that the abilities to bear a healthy child and engage in sexual relations did not constitute "major life activities." Interestingly enough, when the decision rendered in this case was cited by the defense in the case of Benjamin R. v. Orkin Exterminating Co., Inc., in West Virginia several months later, that court found the Burgess decision "unpersuasive."

The court in the Burgess case further cited the concept of employment-at-will and the fact that North Carolina had always been a firm believer in the doctrine as a reason for ignoring public policy arguments supporting a decision in Burgess' favor. This doctrine of employment-at-will was also the primary factor in cases heard in Pennsylvania and Virginia where HIV-positive employees received no protection from the court in their employment discrimination claims.

In the Pennsylvania case of Evans v. Kornfeld, Evans began work for the defendant's hotel in August, 1987 and informed his manager one month later of his homosexuality and HIV seropositivity. While the defendant maintained his physical capability of continuing his job duties, he received a letter of termination the following day. The court rejected his claim of violation of the Pennsylvania Human Relations Act on the ground that his employment was "at-will" and that there was no mandate that he be terminated for "just cause." The court further held that the public policy exception to this rule was not relevant as his discharge was not motivated by any specific intent by his employer to harm him.

In the Virginia case, Chapoton v. Majestic Caterers, the plaintiff was fired by the defendant employer after informing the owner of the company of his asymptomatic HIV-positive status. When Chapoton sued under the Virginia Rights of Persons With Disabilities Act, the court did find asymptomatic HIV infection to be covered under the law but dismissed the claim as "tortious dismissal of an employee-at-will."

In the Ohio case of Doe v. St. Luke's Hospital, the plaintiff, an HIV-positive orthopedic technician, brought suit against his employer, alleging that unauthorized disclosure of his HIV status led to his dismissal by hospital officials. Doe's employee medical records which included his HIV status were shown to managers by hospital staff without his permission, causing hospital officials to discriminate against him. Doe was forced to take medical leave and during this time his position was filled. When he reapplied to his former position, he was denied reinstatement and subsequently placed in a part-time clerk's position with lower pay.

The court found for the defendant hospital and although the reasoning for the court's decision is not available, the verdict in part affirms one previously discussed case and seems to contradict another. In the Kautz v. Humana Hospital–Lucerne case, the finding for the plaintiff stated that the hospital failed to offer Kautz, a surgical technician, another position within the hospital. St. Luke's Hospital's action in this case, filed after Kautz was decided, appears to be consistent with the decision rendered in the Kautz case relative to accomodating employees. St. Luke's, unlike Humana Hospital - Lucerne, did attempt to "accommodate" the employee by placing him in another position. However, in Doe v. Westchester County Medical Center, restrictions on the job duties of a pharmacist were found to be in violation of the law. While the job responsibilities of a pharmacist and those of an orthopedic technician can not be directly compared, it would appear that the risk of HIV transmission within the context of performing the responsibilities of each job would be comparable.

In two separate but similar cases, the United States Navy was found to be in compliance with the Vocational Rehabilitation Act in its treatment of employees who were asymptomatic carriers of HIV. In the case of Doe v. Garrett, Secretary of the Department of the Navy, a naval reservist tested HIV-positive but showed no symptoms of illness. Upon his release from active duty, he brought suit under the Rehabilitation Act alleging discrimination based on handicap. In the case of Doe v. Ball, a naval reserve canvasser recruiter tested positive, was released from active duty, and subsequently brought suit under the Rehabilitation Act. In both cases the courts ruled that the Rehabilitation Act did not apply to uniformed military personnel.

In Doe v. Garrett the court stated that "the statute does not afford a remedy to uniformed military personnel and does not override the military's countervailing statutory authority to prescribe physical qualifications for enlistees." In Doe v. Ball the court stated that "the Rehabilitation

Act's affirmative action mandate requiring each agency within the executive branch to develop programs for hiring, placement and advancement of handicapped individuals did not extend to programs involving military personnel."

While the federal court for the District of Columbia found for the plaintiff in the previously discussed case of Doe v. District of Columbia, a similar case involving a Florida firefighter was judged for the defendant, even though both cases were Rehabilitation Act actions. In Severino v. North Fort Myers Fire Control District, a firefighter who voluntarily resigned after learning he was HIV-positive was subsequently placed on light duty and then discharged after he refused to perform light duty assignments. Severino brought action under the Vocational Rehabilitation Act.

In its ruling the court found for the defendant due to several facts. It stated that the fire district had tried to work out the problem for Severino's benefit by allowing him to return to "light duty," thereby satisfying the requirement of "reasonable accommodation." Severino also failed to present conclusive medical documentation of his ability to perform rescue work, as had been requested by the district. Severino's personal physician had testified that rescue work, which constituted 90% of an on-line firefighter's duties, could not be performed by Severino without risking transmission of the virus. Further, the court reasoned that Severino's hostile conduct toward the Chief of the Department contributed to his termination and that he was not terminated solely for the reason of his handicap; his job conduct was a factor as well.

While the Severino case does illustrate what the courts might construe to be "reasonable accommodation" for an HIV-positive firefighter, its conclusions as to the risk of HIV transmission by a firefighter are in direct conflict with the opinion rendered in Doe v. District of Columbia. Even if the district's belief regarding the necessity of light duty was erroneous in the Severino case, it did rely upon reasonable medical opinion in assigning Severino to light duty, an opinion that was not challenged in the court. Taken together, the Severino case and Doe v. District of Columbia, both decided in 1992, clearly imply that medical opinion regarding the risk of transmission of the virus in certain work settings is neither uniform nor conclusive. Medical opinion can, however, influence an employment discrimination case verdict in favor of either party.

In another case decided in favor of the employer, a vice-president of a commercial real estate firm in Colorado was discharged and filed suit under both federal and state law. In Phelps v. Field Real Estate Company the plaintiff was allegedly discharged due to a reorganization of the company and poor performance of the division he managed. Phelps argued that he was HIV-positive and that his termination was motivated by the

company's desire to deny him insurance benefits. The company responded that it had been previously unaware of his health status and offered
Phelps the chance to stay on as a commissioned real estate agent with
continued benefits. The plaintiff declined and filed suit alleging that his
employer violated the federal Employment Retirement Income Security
Act. He alleged the plaintiff fired him to deny him benefits and that the
company also violated the Colorado Anti-Discrimination Act by firing a
handicapped worker.

The federal court ruled that there was no violation of ERISA because
the decision to terminate Phelps was based on a reorganization and the
poor performance of his division. The court found that no evidence existed to show that the defendant made any calculations as to any increased
costs of benefits or expressed any awareness of such consequences. Also,
it reasoned that motivation was absent due to the fact that the termination was not made until more than 14 months after any initial rumors
concerning the plaintiff's health began circulating. Additional evidence
supported the poor performance of the division, providing a factual
objective basis for the reason given for discharging Phelps. Further,
Phelps had no signs of symptoms of illness prior to the firing.

The state court found that while having AIDS or being HIV-positive
was a handicap within the definition of the Colorado law, liability
required *showing that the employer knew* or should have known of the
physical condition and need to accommodate. It stated that "when an
employee prevents the employer from gaining an awareness of a handicap, there is no liability." The court found the plaintiff to be "manipula-
tive and secretive and to not have functioned as one would have expected a member of a management team."

The Phelps case clearly shows the application of the concept of "business necessity" as a means of circumventing the provisions of laws relating to discrimination of handicapped employees. It also clearly identifies
the need for these employees to assume the burden of notifying their
employers of their handicapped status, validating the defense of "ignorance" to a discrimination claim.

Discussion

The courts have had mixed reactions to employment discrimination
claims filed by HIV-positive asymptomatic individuals. Virtually all of the
state laws rely on definitions from the Vocational Rehabilitation Act and
hence define a handicapped individual identically. However, the interpretations of this definition have been inconsistent. While some courts
have found HIV infection, in and of itself, to constitute a physical impairment, others have not. While some courts have found, HIV infection, in
and of itself, to limit major life activities, others have not. The extent to

which certain occupations, such as firefighting, allow susceptibility of transmission by asymptomatic HIV carriers is still debated by the medical community as well as the courts.

The cases in this section provide some guidance as to what constitutes reasonable accommodation as well as an operational guideline concerning the defense of business necessity. Yet, they are hardly able to present a consistent reading of the law relative to the protection afforded to asymptomatic HIV-positive employees. Given that the Americans With Disabilities Act utilizes many of the same definitions as the laws examined herein, we can expect case law to continue to evolve in this domain. While the ADA does not expressly include HIV infection as a disability, the intent of Congress to include HIV coverage as a disability is clear in its proceedings that discussed the scope of coverage of the Act. Until a small group of precedent-setting cases is heard under the ADA, the likely status of protection for asymptomatic HIV-infected employees remains unclear and may likely vary according to the facts of the particular case.

Cases Involving Individuals with AIDS-Related Complex

Very few cases were found where the plaintiff who had alleged discrimination against his/her employer was classified as having ARC. The probable reason is that many health care professionals have come to believe that the distinction between ARC and full-blown AIDS is, at best, artificial. Clinical parameters as to what constitutes a case of full-blown AIDS have been broadened since the onset of the epidemic. Currently, any individual exhibiting signs of immune system disfunction is said to have AIDS. Nonetheless, an analysis of those cases in which the plaintiff was identified as having ARC may shed some light on some of the issues that will be developing in the future for individuals classified as having full-blown AIDS.

Judgments for the Plaintiff

One of the earliest cases heard relative to HIV and employment was a 1984 case, heard under the Michigan Handicappers Civil Rights Act. In Trueman v. Camden, the plaintiff was a licensed insurance agent hired by the defendant in December, 1983 at which time the parties entered into a two-year employment contract. In March, 1984 Trueman was diagnosed with Karposi's Sarcoma and informed the defendant that he would be going undergoing chemotherapy to treat his condition. The defendant immediately canceled the employment contract, despite the fact that the contract called for a 30-day written cancellation notice.

The court found that the defendant discriminated against Trueman on the basis of his handicap and also was liable for breach of contract. The defendant was awarded reinstatement and an award of back pay pursuant to the terms of the employment contract.

In the case of Club Swamp Annex v. Douglas H. White, a waiter employed by the Club Swamp Annex restaurant was diagnosed with ARC and terminated several weeks later. The reason given for the discharge was that the majority owner of the club "couldn't face" White in the restaurant because of his ARC diagnosis. White sued under the New York State Human Rights Act. The defendant was ordered to reinstate the plaintiff with backpay and compensatory damages. This award included a $5,000 award for mental anguish.

In one of the earlier landmark cases involving an employee with ARC, a long-term employee of a public utility successfully sued his employer under Massachusetts state law. In Cronan v. New England Telephone Co., the plaintiff, a twelve-year employee was diagnosed with ARC in May, 1985. He was forced to disclose the nature of his medical problem by his supervisor and refused, in fear of losing his job. Upon receiving assurance of confidentiality, Cronan informed his supervisor who, in turn, divulged the information to company superiors. Company managers then informed large groups of employees that the plaintiff had AIDS and would be taking disability leave.

A coworker then called the plaintiff to warn him that some fellow workers had threatened to lynch him if he returned to work. At this time several coworkers waited outside the plaintiff's house to harass and threaten him when he walked his dog. Because he feared for his physical safety and was anxious because his privacy had been violated, Cronan did not immediately seek to return to work. When the plaintiff contacted company employment representatives to determine how they should both proceed, the company did not return his repeated calls and placed him on indefinite disability leave. The plaintiff was subsequently diagnosed with PCP and in September, 1985 was diagnosed with full-blown AIDS. He sued his employer for violation of privacy and unlawful discrimination against the handicapped under Massachusetts state law.

The court found that forcing the plaintiff to disclose his medical condition and then publicizing this information to other employees constituted a violation of privacy. In making this determination the court weighed the employer's legitimate business interest against the employee's right to privacy. The court found the employer to be in violation of Massachusetts state law in determining that "the potential to contract other illnesses constituted the handicap" in Cronan's case. The court further stated that an individual with ARC could qualify as a handicapped person based solely on the employer's erroneous perception of him being someone who is contagious to coworkers. Because Cronan was too sick to return to work by the time the case was heard, reinstatement was not a potential remedy. The parties did settle the matter out-of-court with the details of the settlement remaining private.

Judgments for the Defendant

One case was reported in which judgment was rendered for the defendant. In Hilton v. Southwestern Bell Telephone Company, the plaintiff began to work for the defendant company in 1976 and was diagnosed with ARC in October, 1986. Hilton went on disability from November 3, 1986 to September 23, 1987. During this time his personal physician submitted at least twelve separate documents substantiating Hilton's total disability. Hilton attempted to return to work on October 1, 1987 after being on temporary disability for eleven months. Company-paid short-term disability covered a maximum period of twelve months. An independent physician found at this time that Hilton should not return to work. Hilton was then offered permanent disability by the company but sued under the Texas Commission on Human Rights Act for discrimination against a handicapped person.

The court found no evidence that the defendant discriminated on the basis of Hilton's handicap. It reasoned that Hilton's condition did not come under the TCHRA's definition of a handicap because he was not physiologically impaired. The court stated that "the senses, the abilities to walk, use hands and arms, sit or stand are not affected." The court also found that "even though Hilton's condition did not impair his ability to perform his specific functions of work as a drafting clerk, his return to work as a drafting clerk would pose to himself a constant risk of instant death as the slightest jostle could rupture his spleen or otherwise, causing uncontrollable fatal bleeding." The court stated that "the mere act of traveling from home to work and back each day would be death defying. Every trip to the pencil sharpener, to the supply closet, to the restroom, to a supervisor's office, or elsewhere—each a job-related function—is for Hilton a potentially fatal act. In a nutshell, Hilton is totally disabled but not handicapped within the restrictive definition of the Texas Commission on Human Rights Act."

The court clearly ruled that ARC and its related conditions did not constitute handicaps under the TCHRA. However this 1991 verdict seemed to be somewhat contradictory in its finding. While the court found Hilton not to be impaired, it also found the trip to work to be "death defying" in his case.

Discussion

As previously stated, the body of case law pertaining to employees afflicted with ARC is not large, probably due to the aforementioned fact that the clinical term ARC is being phased out. In two of the cases cited above the time between the filing of the complaint and the rendering of the verdict was three years. Therefore it is highly probable that the smaller number of cases was due to the fact that other potential plaintiffs became too sick to continue their cases or saw no reason to pursue reinstatement once their physical conditions deteriorated. Nonetheless, those with ARC have found protection under several state handicap laws.

Cases Involving Individuals with AIDS

Individuals diagnosed with full-blown AIDS who retain the ability to work potentially present one of the greatest challenges to the legal system relative to employment discrimination. While they are healthy enough to maintain their job responsibilities and duties, they often manifest physical symptoms that may cause alarm for coworkers and/or customers. Because of this and the fact that they may inevitably run up significant health care costs that may affect their employer financially, they may be a heightened target for discrimination. At the same time, because their illness is often cyclical in nature, the status of a reasonable accommodation may frequently change. Hence, today's decision may be based on facts that are obsolete by next week. Those with full-blown AIDS also have shortened life expectancies. The cumbersome and often lengthy judicial process may not be worth their while nor an activity toward which they wish to channel what limited physical and mental energies they have.

Judgments for the Plaintiff

Two of the major cases involving a person with full-blown AIDS were previously discussed in Chapter 2. The first, Shuttleworth v. Broward County Office of Budget and Management Policy was a Florida state case where the court ruled that AIDS constitutes a handicap under the Florida Human Rights Act. The second, Chalk v. United States District Court, Central District of California, was a Rehabilitation Act case where the plaintiff, a teacher of hearing-impaired students, received an injunction returning him to the classroom due to the facts that he was "otherwise qualified " to reassume his duties and that his reassignment to a desk job would cause him irreparable injury.

While no other cases have been heard under the Rehabilitation Act, several cases have been heard under state laws that have adopted the Rehabilitation Act definition of a handicapped person. Cain v. Hyatt and Hyatt Legal Services was a case in which the plaintiff was a regional partner of the defendant law firm, Hyatt Legal Services. Within one week of learning of Cain's AIDS diagnosis, senior partner Hyatt fired the plaintiff despite the fact that Cain's physician assured the defendant that Cain would be able to carry out all of his job responsibilities. Despite this, Hyatt felt that over time Cain would become incapable of performing his responsibilities and would hurt the morale of the region's staff due to fear of workplace transmission. Cain remained healthy for nine months subsequent to his dismissal during which time he could have performed his work-related duties without restriction. Cain filed suit, arguing that Hyatt's actions violated the Pennsylvania Human Relations Act prohibiting employment discrimination on the basis of a non-job related handicap or disability.

The court first found that AIDS did constitute a handicap within the meaning of the PHRA for two reasons. First, the disease gives rise to physical symptoms that impair the infected person's ability to engage in major life activities as defined in the Act. Second, persons with AIDS suffer from society's prejudices.

The court also found that the plaintiff's disability was non-job related because it did not substantially interfere with his ability to perform the essential functions of his job. It also found that the employer was obligated not to discriminate against handicapped persons. The rule was not circumvented by Hyatt's other employees' unreasonable fears of that person.

The court also found Hyatt to be in violation of the PHRA as evidence showed that the defendant had been pleased with the plaintiff's job performance up until it was learned that Cain had AIDS. Two raises and a promotion within the previous ten months prior to the discovery of Cain's condition satisfied this requirement for the court.

In a complaint heard by the New York City Commission on Human Rights (In Re A., No. GA-00167020389-DN, July 19, 1990), a retail store owner was found to be in violation of the New York State Human Rights Act in its treatment of an employee with AIDS. The complainant, a longtime employee and manager of a retail store, was being treated for AIDS-related cancer. Despite his sickly appearance, he maintained the ability to fully perform his job responsibilities. He informed his employer that he had cancer but not AIDS, despite the fact that several other store employees were known to have AIDS or be HIV-positive. The employer fired the complainant and replaced him with a person the employer knew to be HIV-positive but asymptomatic. The employer alleged the firing was due to the facts that the complainant was difficult to get along with and a poor worker.

The employer was held liable for discrimination in violation of the NYSHRA and ordered to pay damages for lost wages and emotional distress.

In the case of Raytheon v. California Fair Employment and Housing Commission, Estate of Chadbourne, Real Party in Interest, the federal court rendered a verdict for the defendant. However, a verdict was rendered for the plaintiff under California state law. Chadbourne had been employed as a quality control analyst with a three-year tenure of consistently high evaluations and maximum available raises. When he came down with PCP, he was hospitalized and diagnosed with AIDS. Upon his release, his physician, an infectious disease specialist, provided a letter stating that Chadbourne was fully able to return to his job and posed no threat of contagion. Raytheon refused to allow Chadbourne to return to work despite the agreement among Chadbourne's personal physician, the United States Department of Health and Human Services, the United States Centers for Disease Controls, the Santa Barbara County Health Services, and Raytheon's own medical staff that there was no risk of transmission to coworkers. Despite overwhelming medical opinion that there was no risk of transmission, Raytheon's medical director recommended Chadbourne not be allowed to return to work and that the company "beg for time."

Chadbourne sought administrative relief and filed complaints with both the federal Office of Federal Contracts Compliance Programs and the California Fair Employment and Housing Commission. The OFCCP found no discrimination. The rationale for the decision is not available. The state commission, however, found Raytheon to be in violation of state law. It found Chadbourne to be handicapped and otherwise qualified as defined by California's Fair Employment and Housing Act. It also found that where a handicap is a contagious disease, an employee remains otherwise qualified if he/she is capable of working without putting co-workers at risk of contagion. The commission found the defendant's concerns about contagion to be erroneous since HIV is not transmitted by casual contact. Hence, the defendant's refusal to permit Chadbourne to return to work constituted unlawful discrimination. Damages were awarded to Chadbourne's estate as he had died in the interim.

In Raytheon's appeal of the decision to the California Supreme Court, the finding of the lower court was upheld. The Supreme Court ruled that a physical handicap included any bodily condition that has a disabling effect and that such disabling effect need not be immediate. It rejected the argument by the defendant that when Chadbourne was refused reinstatement, little was known about AIDS. The court concluded that the evidence presented contradicted this and that the company could not prove Chadbourne to be a risk to his co-workers.

Two cases involving the termination of employees with AIDS were related to potential health insurance costs. In Doe v. Cooper Investment, the plaintiff was fired after informing his employer that he had AIDS. The plaintiff alleged that the firing was to avoid additional costs which would result from his use of the company health insurance plan. He was told he would have to pay the costs of his health insurance premium if he wished to retain coverage after termination. When he was unable to do so, the policy was canceled. The court found the defendant employer in violation of the Employee Retirement Income Security Act because it fired the employee in an attempt to avoid providing health benefits and the judge issued a restraining order directing Cooper Investment to provide the plaintiff with health insurance. The parties later settled out-of-court with the plaintiff receiving $50,000 cash and $25,000 in additional insurance coverage.

The other case related to health insurance involved an alleged violation of the Texas Commission on Human Rights Act. In Gardner v. Rainbow Lodge, the plaintiff who had AIDS was an employee of the defendant's bar, which employed 30-40 people. When the bar's owner sought new health insurance, one insurer said it would insure the group except for Gardner. The insurer rejected Gardner because he had a history of hepatitis—not because he had AIDS. The owner refused the offer but soon thereafter fired Gardner allegedly for tardiness and "other infractions." The day following his termination, the owner signed up with the insurance company. Gardner claimed his termination was discriminatory and illegal under the TCHRA. A jury found for Gardner in the case, holding that the defendant had wrongly terminated Gardner and awarded him $60,000 for back wages and emotional suffering.

Judgments for the Defendant

In Estate of Behringer v. Medical Center at Princeton, an otolaryngologist and plastic surgeon was diagnosed with AIDS by the hospital at which he was a member of the staff and had surgical privileges. The hospital first imposed conditions on his continued performance of surgical procedures at the hospital, requiring him to obtain informed consent of any patients, but later totally revoked these same surgical privileges. Behringer brought suit against the hospital alleging employment discrimination based on handicap.

The court found the medical center not to be in violation of the New Jersey Law Against Discrimination. It stated that restricting the plaintiff's surgical privileges was substantially justified by a "reasonable probability" of harm to patients. The "risk of harm" included not only actual transmission but the risk of a surgical accident (i.e., scalpel cut or needle stick). It further found that the medical center's policy of restricting the surgical privileges of health care providers who pose "any risk of HIV transmission to the patient" was a "reasonable exercise of the medical center's authority as applied to the facts of this case, where the plaintiff was an AIDS-infected surgeon."

The major significance of this case was that it addressed the risk factor associated with certain types of employment. In reaching its verdict the court addressed the apparent conflict between a physician's rights under handicap employment discrimination law and a patient's "right to know" under the doctrine of "informed consent."

In a Rehabilitation Act case, a postal worker charged his employer with discrimination based on his handicap of AIDS. In Ritter v. United States Postal Service, the plaintiff had received several disciplinary actions due to his continued AWOL (absent without leave) status and for failing to comply with the rules governing absences which required a telephone call or "some other notification." Upon being terminated the plaintiff argued that he lived alone and had no telephone. The plaintiff also waited until filing his discrimination suit to allege *for the first time* that his dismissal constituted handicap discrimination based on his AIDS condition.

The court found no violation of the Rehabilitation Act since none of the medical evidence presented supported the dates of misconduct (absence) and the plaintiff provided no evidence of his being incapacitated at those times. In other words, the plaintiff could not connect his alleged illness to the misconduct displayed on the dates charged. The plaintiff presented no evidence showing that his medical condition caused his absences or his failure to comply with the agency's rules and regulations governing absences. The court also stated that an employee who asserts a charge of handicap discrimination must show that the alleged discriminator possessed knowledge of the handicapping condition. As in the previously discussed cases of Petri v. Bank of New York Co. Inc., and Rose City Oil v. Missouri Commission on Human Rights, the court found that a defendant could not be held liable for any alleged discrimination if the said defendant had no knowledge of the employee's handicap.

Two of the most publicized cases regarding employment discrimination based on AIDS heard in 1992 were cases that had to do health insurance benefits and alleged violations of the Employee Retirement Income Security Act. The first was Owens v. Storehouse, Inc.. In this case the plaintiff participated in an employee welfare benefits plan sponsored by the defendant employer which provided group medical and hospitalization benefits. When the financial condition of both the plan and the company deteriorated, the defendant modified the plan to cap or limit AIDS-related medical benefits at $25,000 and provided the plaintiff, who had AIDS at the time, an additional $7,500 as a "transitional benefit." Owens filed a suit alleging that the employer's cap violated ERISA regulations and that Storehouse, Inc. had breached its fiduciary duty under ERISA.

The court found that the cap was not in violation of ERISA in stating that statutory language, legislative history and case law all made clear that ERISA was designed to protect the "employment relationship" and not the integrity of the specific benefit plan. ERISA specifically states that "It shall be unlawful for any person to discharge, fine, suspend, expel, discipline, or discriminate against a participant or beneficiary for exercising any right to which he is entitled under the provision of an employee benefit plan." The court found that ERISA was not the appropriate vehicle for addressing the unilateral elimination of nonvested benefits *accomplished independently of employee termination or harassment.* Since the allegations fail to raise the issue of discrimination against the "employment relationship," that ERISA was designed to protect, the plaintiff's claim was ruled to be invalid. In other words, the court stated that ERISA allowed an employer to restrict benefits to employees as long as the employees were not fired or harassed. The court also failed to find the defendant in breach of its fiduciary responsibility under ERISA as it found that ERISA allows an employer to consider "business needs" in modifying a benefit plan.

The second case, McGann v. H & H Music Co., had a similar outcome based on similar judicial reasoning despite slightly different facts. McGann claimed that the defendant employer discriminated against him because he had AIDS by switching the company's insurance coverage to a self-insurance plan that reduced the cap on AIDS-related benefits from $1 million to $5,000. McGann alleged that the employer changed the plan in response to the plaintiff's claim for benefits, in violation of ERISA.

The court found the defendant not to be in violation of ERISA. It reasoned that revisions in the employer's AIDS insurance coverage were done to preserve the insurance plan after it had suffered serious losses from other AIDS claims. The court held that H & H had the right to change the plan and that McGann did not have a right to health benefits whose terms never changed. The court further found that the defendant had complied with ERISA by serving the employees with written notices of the revisions in their insurance plan. It also reasoned that the reduction of AIDS benefits was not intended to deny benefits to McGann for any reason that would not also be applicable to other beneficiaries of the plan who might then or thereafter have AIDS. Rather, the reduction was prompted by the knowledge of McGann's illness and that McGann happened to be the only beneficiary then known to have AIDS.

Discussion

For the most part, the reviewed cases have shown individuals with full-blown AIDS to be protected from discrimination in employment due to their handicap. The cases judged in favor of the defendants generally had extenuating circumstances (i.e., a practicing surgeon and an insubordinate employee who did not have obvious signs of infection nor inform his employer of his alleged disability). It appears however, that one area of future contention will involve whether full health insurance benefits will be continued for those with AIDS. The Employee Retirement Income Security Act does not mandate that employee welfare benefit plans be maintained nor does it restrict employers from self-insuring their employees. In either cases, the maximum dollar amount for any illness may be capped at any time as long as that cap applies to all employees.

The ADA may not affect this issue significantly as the provisions in the ADA which govern insurance are ambiguous at best. Section 501 (c) of the Act exempts "insurers...or any entity that administers benefits plans...that are not inconsistent with State law." Hence, while the ADA prohibits employers from discriminating based on handicap, it allows insurers to do so as long as they do not violate state law in assessing underwriting risks. ERISA remains the only federal law that provides a defense against discrimination charges by companies that self-insure. Indeed, in the McGann case the court found that ERISA afforded no protection to the employee. Because the United States Supreme Court has refused to hear an appeal of the McGann case, the decision in McGann has become law in the Fifth Circuit, consisting of the states of Louisiana, Texas and Mississippi. It further sets a precedent for other circuits to follow.

The importance of this issue can not be overstated. The number of cases of HIV infection is increasing. Newer therapies are prolonging the lives of both those carrying the virus and those with full-blown AIDS. The overall health care costs of caring for a society will continue to increase. Absent the willingness of private insurers and employers to assume their share of the burden of these costs, further stress will be placed on already overburdened and fiscally weak health care and public assistance systems.

4

Means of Discrimination

Employers have discriminated in a variety of ways against workers infected or perceived to be infected with HIV. This chapter extends the analysis from the previous chapter by looking at the various forms of discrimination (specific discriminatory behaviors and actions) that employers have used. All classes of HIV infection are grouped together within each particular means of discrimination. This facilitates an analysis of how the courts are dealing with the general types of discrimination and a determination of which types of discrimination are generally the most actionable.

Discriminatory Behaviors

Disclosure of Test Results

At present, no federal law or policy guarantees an individual infected with HIV the specific right to privacy. Many individual states, however, are beginning to address the issue by developing their own laws. Consequently, under the doctrine of invasion of privacy, an employer could be sued by an employee who was HIV-positive if the employer disclosed this status without the employee's consent. An employee who was HIV-negative but believed to be positive or one who received an erroneous HIV-positive test result could have the grounds sue an employer for defamation of character if such test results were revealed. The potential defamation or liability could result from the implication that the individual was a homosexual or drug user. The employee could allege that he or she suffered emotional distress as a result of the disclosure.

There are, however, limitations to this doctrine. In the non-HIV case of Oil, Chemical & Atomic Workers Local Union No. 6-418 v. the National Labor Relations Board, the union contended that in order to bargain effectively with employers over health and safety issues, it needed access to various company records including health information obtained through workers' compensation and insurance claims. The court held that if employers could delete from their records names and any other information that could link the record to a specific employee, releasing this information would not violate the employees' rights to privacy.

Closely related to this issue of confidentiality and disclosure is the question of whether employers should be allowed to test current or prospective employees for HIV. Traditionally, there were three grounds on which private sector employers attempted to justify such testing. They were 1) to identify those who would be unable to work in the future, 2) to determine whether job conditions posed a serious threat to co-workers or customers' health and safety, and 3) to screen potential employees to assess potential health care costs.

Section 102 (c)(4) of the Americans With Disabilities Act clearly prohibits such inquiries unless all employees receive the same test and the employer can prove that the testing is relevant to a specific job-related function. In other words, all employees would have to be tested for HIV, regardless of the employer's perceptions of a specific current or prospective employee's risk for infection. As previously discussed, however, employers are allowed to assess the risk factor involved for those employees that they themselves insure, leaving a gaping hole in the testing provisions which the ADA attempts to limit. Under the ADA, the ability of insurers to continue to utilize HIV test results to make determinations as to coverage limitation and exclusions has the potential to perpetuate widespread discrimination against those with HIV infection.

When asked to evaluate the legality of HIV testing to a specific job-related function, the courts have generally been sympathetic to employees. In the case of Cronan v. New England Telephone Co., the court found that the employer violated the plaintiff's right to privacy under Massachusetts state law. The courts also judged against employer's actions in the cases of Sanchez v. Lagoudakis, Buler v. Southland Corp., d/b/a/ Seven-Eleven Stores, and State of Minnesota v. Di Ma Corporation and Richard Carriveau where employers required employees to present the results of HIV tests as a condition of continued employment. Although in each of these three latter cases, the testing was not a specific violation of state law (and not in violation of federal law because the cases preceded the ADA), the courts found the testing unnecessary and a contributing factor in assessing the employer's liability in each case.

Employees have found mixed protection in this regard in health care settings. In Estate of Behringer v. Medical Center at Princeton, the court found that the hospital had breached its duty to keep the patient/employee's records private. The court argued that disclosure by any employer, even a health care institution, is not allowed. However, in Leckelt v. Board of Commissioners of Hospital District No. 1, the courts found that requiring test results of the plaintiff nurse was not in violation of either Louisiana state law or the Vocational Rehabilitation Act given the potential risk of transmission. The clear implication here is that an assessment of job-related risk in health care settings is still in a state of development. While the Centers for Disease Control have issued precautionary guidelines for health care workers and encouraged practitioners to utilize informed consent in treating patients, interpretation of the law relative to health care workers is still open.

In another setting, the court did define the validity of job-related testing. In Local 1812, American Federation of Government Employees v. United States Department of State, the court found that foreign service employees who were HIV-infected were handicapped within the meaning of the Rehabilitation Act but that they were not otherwise qualified for worldwide duty. The court based its conclusion on the fact that HIV-infected employees would be subject to poor medical care and unsanitary conditions in many foreign posts and that these conditions would be harmful to them due to their impaired immune systems. The court also ruled that testing of such employees was permissible because no employee would be terminated or denied benefits as a result of testing positive. Asymptomatics, the court reasoned, could be posted to countries with "safe" health and sanitary conditions.

In sum, under the ADA broad pre-employment testing for HIV is prohibited. Employers are permitted to offer employment conditioned on an applicant being willing to submit to a medical examination which includes an HIV test. The test, however, must be given to all applicants, the results must be kept confidential, and the results cannot be used to justify withdrawing a conditional employment offer unless the test results can show that the applicant is, in fact, not qualified for the job. In addition, most states do require informed written consent prior to testing anyone for the HIV virus. Seven states (California, Florida, Maine, Massachusetts, Texas, Vermont and Wisconsin) have made it unlawful for employers to demand HIV antibody tests of any applicants for employment or current employees unless it can be demonstrated that there is a legitimate bona fide occupational qualification for doing so. Because most of these state laws are relatively new, a body of case law has yet to be established to determine what occupations or circumstances would qualify under the condition of "bona fide occupational qualification." Given the above discussion of the Behringer and Leckelt cases, it is likely that health care occupations might constitute a "gray" area in this regard, requiring the courts' interpretations.

It is somewhat ironic that testing designed to screen out HIV applicants might have the opposite effect. By making public the handicapping status the applicant or employee might otherwise not choose to reveal, the applicant or employee is given grounds for a discrimination suit which might otherwise be meritless without employer knowledge. This was evidenced in the cases of Petri v. Bank of New York Co., Inc., Phelps v. Field Real Estate Company, and Rose City Oil Company v. Missouri Commission on Human Rights. Rulings in these cases would provide an incentive for employers not to test to support a potential defense of ignorance against a discrimination charge.

Insurance Cancellations/Modifications

There has not been a significant number of cases of alleged discrimination relative to an employer's denial of insurance benefits. In fact, all but one of the cases found are recent (since 1991). It may be that this form of employment discrimination represents a new trend, a reasonable conclusion when one considers the terms of the ADA; it has very broad and far-reaching provisions prohibiting employment discrimination, yet exempts insurers from its regulations.

The insurance industry charges different rates to different individuals based upon expected losses under the issued policies. This process of risk classification is considered essential by the insurance industry for its financial well-being. Insurers determine the expected losses on each policyholder and place individuals with similar expected losses into the same classification so that all may be charged at the same rate. The problem one faces when dealing with health insurance for workers infected with HIV is one of balancing the basis upon which the insurance industry is built and functions while simultaneously furthering societal values and principles and laws concerning nondiscrimination.

A number of reasons have been presented to oppose HIV testing by insurers. One of the most prominent is the fact that the initial test is not totally reliable. False results can necessarily give rise to additional discrimination against members of certain high-risk groups. Further, tested individuals may have their privacy rights violated, and perhaps most important, such testing may actually endanger public health. Individuals may not undertake voluntary testing which assists in both early treatment of those infected and in helping to limit the further spread of the virus, because they fear they may not qualify for insurance based on prior HIV test results.

Nonetheless, the insurance industry and its advocates have provided reasons to support HIV testing by insurers. They include the necessities of keeping the insurance industry intact and the desire for consistency in treating HIV in the same manner as other diseases for which the industry tests. They argue that prohibitions on AIDS testing will completely force insurers out of many markets where insurance coverage is needed the most, particularly in large cities. Furthermore, prohibitions on testing will force the healthy general public to unreasonably bear a disproportionate amount of HIV-related insurance expenses.

Facts relating to the justification of HIV testing by insurers are mixed. Medical evidence shows that over a seven year span a person infected with HIV is 26 times more likely to die than an individual with "standard risks." However, as of 1988, payments for AIDS claims had not exceeded 1% of all health and life insurance payments and are not projected to exceed 10% of the same for the foreseeable future. It has also been argued that HIV testing by insurers is clearly cost-ineffective. One insurance company CEO has calculated that it would cost his company $450,000 per week to test all applicants for HIV yet the average medical claim relative to AIDS is only $75,000 over the life of the patient.

The courts have not allowed employers to refuse employment to those at risk for insurance claims nor to discharge an employee on the belief that his/her condition might result in benefit claims. In Chrysler Outboard Corporation v. Wisconsin Department of Industry, the court found the refusal to hire an applicant with acute lymphocytic leukemia was a violation of the Rehabilitation Act. In the case of Folz v. Marriott Corporation, the court found the discharge of an employee with multiple sclerosis was a violation of the Employee Retirement Income Security Act due to the employer's belief that the disease would increase company benefit costs.

Section 510 of ERISA forbids employers from disciplining or discharging employees because they have filed claims for benefits to which they are entitled under an employee benefit plan. Congress amended ERISA in 1986 with what are known as the COBRA amendments. These amendments provide that employers with work forces larger than 20 are obligated to allow discharged employees to continue as participants in their group health insurance plans for up to 18 months, with conversion privileges to individual coverage available at the end of this time. The significance of this relative to HIV is that even if an employer finds a way within the law to discharge an employee infected with HIV who requires medical care, the employer's "experience rating" for risk assessment purposes will continue to be affected even after the discharge.

Alexander v. Choate was a major 1985 Supreme Court decision that laid the framework for case law decisions relative to employee benefits. In this decision the Court held that a state may place durational limits on in-patient coverage in state medicaid plans, despite the resulting disproportionate impact on certain handicapped individuals. They reasoned that as long as the handicapped had equal access to the benefit and the limitation was neutral on its face, there was no violation of federal law.

This decision laid the groundwork for employers being able to put neutral ceilings (those appearing to be free of bias) on benefit packages in order to avoid bearing the health care burdens of those with HIV infection. While it would result in a form of discrimination that was allowed by law, it could also result in less illegal workplace discrimination relative to termination. Employers who could legally restrict benefits might be less prone to terminate an employee with any form of HIV infection.

Employees with HIV infection have found very limited protection in the courts relative to the maintenance of their employer-provided insurance benefits. In one early (1987) case, employees found protection based on a reasoning that would probably not be rendered today. In Doe v. Beaverton Nissan & M.F. Satter, Inc., an Oregon court ruled that an employer's total exclusion of AIDS-related treatment from the company health insurance coverage violated state anti-discrimination law. The decision was based on the fact that 90% of persons with AIDS at that time were male and that the exclusion was seen to be a form of sex discrimination. In rendering its verdict, the court rejected the defendant's arguments that the AIDS exclusion provision affected only a subgroup of males, namely gay males and that the epidemiology of the disease in Africa indicated that AIDS and HIV-infection were not limited to males.

In the previously discussed case of Gardner v. Rainbow Lodge, the court ruled in favor of the plaintiff employee when he was discharged one day prior to his employer's changing insurance carriers. The new carrier had previously refused to insure Gardner due to his history of hepatitis, preventing the employer from contracting the carrier. The court found in Gardner's favor as it reasoned that his termination was "clearly and exclusively" motivated by the desire to deny him benefits.

While Gardner's case set an important precedent, it is apt to be less applicable to some of the cases that are beginning to appear. While employers are clearly prohibited under ERISA from discharging employees to deny them their benefits, there are no laws that prevent employers from altering or revoking benefits from employees *who are not terminated*. This can be clearly illustrated in the previously discussed case of Owens v. Storehouse, Inc. The court ruled that the key mandate of ERISA was the maintenance of the "employment relationship" and not the maintenance of the specific features of the employee benefit plan. It found that ERISA did not outlaw elimination of nonvested benefits accomplished independently of employee termination or harassment. Hence, employers were allowed to restrict benefits to employees who were not "discharged, fined, suspended, expelled, disciplined, or discriminated against."

Similarly, in McGann v. H & H Music, the court ruled that revisions to an employer's AIDS insurance coverage done to preserve the plan after it had suffered serious losses from other AIDS claims were not unlawful. Nothing in ERISA or elsewhere prohibited employers from changing the terms of employee benefits pertaining to welfare, rather than vested, benefits as employees did not have a right to health benefits whose terms never change. As long as the terms of the revised coverage were uniformly applied to all employees, there was no discrimination. This precedent was upheld in the case of Beavers v. Storehouse, Inc. where the court found no ERISA violation when the employer modified its health insurance plan to limit coverage of AIDS and AIDS-related conditions from $ 1 million to $25,000.

Given that insurers need to assess risk in their underwriting practices, legislatures have been reluctant to impose stringent anti-discrimination regulations upon them. However, these exemptions from laws which apply to employers appear to be a major public policy issue for the years ahead. They raise the issue that employers who self-insure can not discriminate as employers but can potentially discriminate as insurers. Unfortunately the ADA has not provided any guidelines as to how this legal dilemma is to be resolved. It will probably take some time for a body of case law to be developed in this area since the ADA's provisions did not go into effect until July 26, 1992.

A related issue involves the question that if private insurance, provided through employment, will not have to bear the costs of HIV-related illness, who will? Since most Americans with health insurance have their policies through their employers, public assistance appears to be the only alternative at this point. It is doubtful that public assistance funds are or will be sufficient to bear this burden indefinitely.

Refusal to Hire or Reinstate

Another area in which employers discriminated against employees, or prospective employees, is in the refusal to reinstate or hire them. Since we now know that the virus can not be transmitted through casual contact, cases in which employers refused to hire or reinstate someone infected with HIV might logically be dated cases, filed and heard in the earlier years of the epidemic. However, the majority of the cases involve claims from 1987 up to the present. In all cases, judgment was rendered for the plaintiff employee or an out-of-court settlement was reached. Hence, the courts have been very responsive to the claims of applicants for employment who allege rejection based on HIV status.

In the case of Doe v. Delta Airlines, a former employee of Pan Am alleged he was denied a job with Delta because he was an HIV-positive gay male. Interestingly, the court found that Delta made unlawful inquiries into the plaintiff's sexual orientation, HIV status, and marital status while screening applications from hundreds of former Pan Am employees. The verdict in this case reflects the previously discussed assertion that what an employer asks may be used as evidence in a legal proceeding. The court's decision was based on these inquiries, making it likely that the applicant would not have had as much success in his suit had the employer just "assumed" the applicant's sexual orientation and HIV status and rejected him. The parties settled out-of-court. The plaintiff was hired with back pay and awarded a modest damage settlement. In addition, Delta established a "working group" to review the airline's employment policies.

In the case of Rice v. Bloomer, the plaintiff was a certified full-time school instructor employed by the defendant school board. After Rice was diagnosed with AIDS, the board placed him on disability leave with full pay and benefits. Two months later when the plaintiff sought medical clearance to return to work, the Board refused to reinstate him. The plaintiff sued the school board under the Rehabilitation Act. A settlement was reached in which the school board promised to maintain the plaintiff's full salary and benefits "indefinitely" in exchange for the plaintiff's relinquishing his right to return to the classroom.

On the surface, the extent to which either party can claim a "victory" in Rice v. Bloomer is dubious at best. However, it is important to remember that the Rehabilitation Act and ADA both mandate that workers remain "otherwise qualified" to perform their duties in order to remain protected under the law. Once Rice became incapacitated, he would no longer have had a cause for action against the school board, leaving him without income and health benefits. While Rice did relinquish his rights to return to his job, this might have been a very small price to pay, given the state of his infection and the potential for his disqualification at any point in the future.

In three previously discussed cases, the courts ruled in favor of plaintiffs who were denied an initial appointment to a position or reinstatement to their former position. In Raytheon v. California Fair Employment and Housing Commission, Estate of Chadbourne, Real Party in Interest, Raytheon was found to be in violation of the Rehabilitation Act by not allowing Chadbourne to return to his job despite the reassurances of numerous health officials that Chadbourne posed no risk of transmission to coworkers. The case, unfortunately, was not finally settled until after Chadbourne's death due to the appellate process.

In Doe v. District of Columbia, an HIV-positive firefighter, who was told not to report for his first day of work, successfully sued the District under the Rehabilitation Act. The court found that the risk of transmission was comparable "to that of being struck by a meteor" and that there were no reported cases of transmission by firefighting or emergency medical personnel through their job duties. However, it is important to remember that in Severino v. North Fort Myers Fire Control District, the court did find that firefighters posed a risk of transmission in their normal duties.

In Doe v. Westchester County Medical Center, the HIV-positive pharmacist who had a job offer revoked when his antibody status was discovered, successfully sued the medical center under both the New York State Human Rights Act and the Vocational Rehabilitation Act. As previously noted, the center's refusal to hire Doe according to the court's mandate jeopardized its annual funding of $107 million from the Department of Health and Human Services.

Employees or prospective employees who have been refused employment or reassignment have generally received significant support from the courts. The ADA codifies this support by declaring all HIV-infection to be a protected handicap for employment purposes. However, it must be remembered that the ADA also mandates that individuals be "otherwise qualified" for the positions and that the Act does provide limitations as to what constitutes "reasonable accommodation" of such employees on the part of employers.

Termination

By far the greatest number of discrimination cases involve an employee who was terminated due to his or her HIV status or perceived HIV status. In the vast majority of these cases, the courts clearly concluded that the various manifestations of HIV infection constituted a protected handicap and, in most cases, even the perception of HIV infection constituted a protected handicap.

A key issue addressed in the majority of these cases was whether there was proof that the defendant was *aware* of the employee's HIV status. If proof existed the employee in question became a member of a protected class for statutory purposes. This was a pertinent fact in a number of cases including Connecticut Human Rights Commission v. Respondent, In Re D., No. GA-0024030987-DN of the New York City Commission on Human Rights, and Jensen v. Casa Toltec.

In Cain v. Hyatt and Hyatt Legal Services, Club Swamp Annex v. Douglas H. White, and State of Minnesota v. Di Ma Corporation and Richard Carriveau, the courts also found that AIDS did not interfere with the plaintiff's ability to perform the essential functions of his job and that an employer's obligation not to discriminate against handicapped persons was not circumvented by the employer's or other employee's unreasonable fears of that person. In both Cain and Shuttleworth v. Broward County Office of Budget and Management Policy, the courts also considered the recent outstanding performance evaluations and merit raises that the plaintiffs had received.

In Kautz v. Humana Hospital–Lucerne, the courts considered the fact that the hospital did not provide the plaintiff with the usual internal review procedures prior to termination and that the hospital did not attempt to find Kautz another position within the facility. In two cases, Gardner v. Rainbow Lodge and Doe v. Cooper Investment, the courts found the employers intended to terminate the employees to deprive them of health care benefits.

The cases in which the courts have upheld the dismissal of employees with HIV or those perceived to have HIV infection have largely been procedural. In both Doe v. Ball and Doe v. Garrett courts upheld the dismissals of naval reservists from active duty since the military forces are exempt from the provisions of the Rehabilitation Act. In the cases of Chapoton v. Majestic Caterers, Burgess v. Your House of Raleigh, Inc., and Evans v. Kornfield, the dismissals of the plaintiffs were found to be within the doctrine of employment-at-will, despite the fact that all three plaintiffs were infected with HIV. Such a defense would probably no longer hold up under the provision of the ADA. The court in the Burgess case also considered the fact that under the North Carolina Handicapped Persons Protection Act, communicable diseases were expressly excluded from coverage. That law has, however, since been amended to include protection for those infected with HIV.

In a significant number of cases, dismissals were upheld because the employee had not tested positive for HIV despite being suspect or had tested positive and not informed his or her employer. For these reasons, the courts found that a handicap had not been established in judging for the defendant employers in the cases of Rose City Oil v. Missouri Commission on Human Rights, Petri v. Bank of New York, Leckelt v. Board of Commissioners of Hospital District No. 1, and Phelps v. Field Real Estate Company. (In the Leckelt case, a further issue involved the fact that the plaintiff, a health care worker, could not establish that he remained "otherwise qualified.")

In the Field case, the court also cited the fact that the plaintiff prevented the employer from discovering his HIV condition as being critical in its finding for the defendant. However, in Hummer v. Unemployment Appeals Commission, the court found that Hummer's lack of disclosure of his HIV infection to management was designed to protect his privacy. Unlike the court in the Field case, the court in the Hummer case did not find the failure to disclose a reason to invalidate an employee's claim. The court ruled that this failure to disclose did not constitute negligence on the part of Hummer and hence, was not a justifiable cause for dismissal. Similarly, in Estate of McKinley v. Boston Harbor Hotel, the commission rejected the defendant's argument that McKinley's failure to tell management about his condition rendered him unprotected by the Massachusetts Fair Employment Act.

The case evidence presented above demonstrates that there is strong support for plaintiffs who have had their employment terminated due to their real or perceived HIV status. Clearly, however, a chief area of contention between plaintiffs and defendants appears to be whether an individual who has not notified his or her employer of a positive HIV status is protected under the law. The courts have been mixed in their response to this question. While the ADA expressly protects those who are perceived as being handicapped, several decisions rendered in favor of employers have involved employer perceptions that had not been confirmed by employee disclosures. An employee would evidently strengthen his or her cause of action by informing the employer of HIV status, hence removing any doubt as to whether that employee was considered disabled for statutory purposes and would fall within the protection offered by the ADA.

Employees must therefore weigh the potential risks of disclosing their HIV status to employers against the protection the disclosure would potentially supply. Medical advances are allowing persons infected with HIV to remain asymptomatic longer, live longer and hence, remain "otherwise qualified" to retain their jobs for longer periods of time. The protection afforded by disclosure could be invaluable.

Reassignment

The ADA requires employers to make "reasonable accommodations" towards the handicaps of employees and applicants. One potential accommodation presented in section 101 (9)(B) involves reassignment to another position. Such accommodations may be refused by an employer if they present an "undue hardship" to the employer as outlined in section 101 (10)(A)-(B). What constitutes a reassignment or any other accommodation being "reasonable" as well as what constitutes an "undue hardship" clearly depends on the facts of the case.

Another dimension of reassignment involves employees who are involuntarily reassigned due to their handicaps. To the extent to which these individuals remain "otherwise qualified" to perform the responsibilities of their original positions, such reassignment may be in violation of the ADA.

The majority of cases involving reassignment or requests for reassignment have been judged in favor of the plaintiff. In Chalk v. United States District Court, Central District of California, Orange County Superintendent of Schools, Chalk's unwelcome reassignment from a classroom teaching position to a desk job upon his AIDS diagnosis was found to be in violation of the Vocational Rehabilitation Act. Despite the fact that the reassigned position was at the same rate of pay, the court found that the reassignment would cause Chalk irreparable injury psychologically in depriving him from the "tremendous personal joy and satisfaction" he received from his classroom work. The court also found that Chalk remained "otherwise qualified" to maintain his teaching responsibilities despite his diagnosis.

Although McKinley was not technically reassigned to another position, his estate received a judgment in its favor in its suit against the Boston Harbor Hotel. When the dining room managers of the hotel began to suspect that McKinley might be suffering from AIDS, as evidenced by their inquiries to McKinley's coworkers, they reassigned him to the least desirable stations in the restaurant and provided him with fewer tables than usual despite his consistent superior performance evaluations.

Two other state cases concerning reassignment were decided in favor of the plaintiffs. In Iacono v. Town of Huntington Security Division, the plaintiff was employed as a commuter railroad station guard. Upon being diagnosed with AIDS he was reassigned to a location without heat or bathroom facilities and had his use of a town-owned car and gasoline rescinded. In Racine Education Association v. Racine Unified School District, members of a teacher's association challenged their school district's policy under the Wisconsin Fair Employment Act to exclude from work staff members with HIV and to place these individuals on sick leave until further work assignments were decided. The teacher's union successful argued that the policy was discriminatory because it required employees to use sick leave and then to take leave without pay when they were fully able to work and did not create a risk of contagion to their students or coworkers. The ruling stated that persons with AIDS are handicapped under state law and that the policy was based on the erroneous assumption that AIDS could be transmitted by casual contact. It also found the policy to be in violation of a state law prohibiting discrimination based on sexual orientation. The court found its goal was to exclude homosexuals from teaching positions.

In several previously discussed cases, the courts ruled in favor of the defendants relative to reassignment decisions. In Estate of Behringer v. Medical Center at Princeton, an otolaryngolist and plastic surgeon had his surgical privileges restricted due to a reasonable probability of harm to a patient. The court found that "any risk of HIV transmission to the patient" rendered the surgeon to not be "otherwise qualified" under the New Jersey Law Against Discrimination.

In Rose City Oil Co. v. Missouri Commission on Human Rights, the court found that a convenience store clerk who was believed to be HIV-positive and reassigned from sandwich making duties to cashiering was not discriminated against under the Missouri Human Rights Act as his job description included both duties. Further, despite the fact that his previous responsibilities almost exclusively involved sandwich making, the reassignment did not result in a pay cut or any substantive change in working conditions.

In the case of Severino v. North Fort Myers Fire Control District, the court found that a firefighter who was reassigned to "light duty" when he tested HIV-positive did not have a cause of action under the Vocational Rehabilitation Act. The court reasoned that rescue work, which constituted 90% of a firefighter's duties could not be performed by Severino without risking transmission of the virus. This case did raise the question of what constitutes "reasonable accommodation" but, as previously stated, is also at odds with the decision rendered in Doe v. District of Columbia.

While both the Rehabilitation Act and the ADA have mandated that employers must make reasonable accommodations to employees or applicants with handicaps/disabilities, it remains to be seen what degree of protection employees have from unwelcome reassignment. A key factor appears to be the extent to which employees remain "otherwise qualified" to perform their job duties. However, in some instances such a conclusion is not easily reached. The debate over whether firefighters pose a risk of transmission is a clear example of this ambiguity. Certain jobs in the medical field as well as the tasks assigned to certain positions may also be scrutinized in this regard. While the Centers for Disease Control have issued guidelines concerning precautions that health care workers can take to significantly minimize the risk of transmission, the regular presence of exposed wounds and cuts and bodily fluids keeps both employees and patients of health care facilities highly concerned.

Summary

The above discussion demonstrates that employees carrying or perceived to be carrying the HIV virus have generally received favorable treatment in the court system. Because the ADA clearly classifies HIV infection as a protected handicap, asymptomatic HIV carriers as well as those diagnosed with ARC and full-blown AIDS may find more protection than they have in the past from employment discrimination. It is worth noting that the legislative history of the ADA involves the use of the term "HIV disease" rather than asymptomatic HIV-positive, ARC, and AIDS. This reflects the revised medical view that the disease does not necessarily develop in a predictable, continuous, linear manner. As previously noted, the singular term HIV disease encompasses an entire spectrum of HIV-related conditions from carrier status to those with terminally-impaired immune systems.

For many of those cases in which a verdict was rendered for the defendant and the plaintiffs were actually infected with the virus, the same case brought under the ADA might now be judged for the plaintiff. Indeed, section 2 of the ADA clearly expresses Congress' dissatisfaction with the level of protection afforded individuals with disabilities prior to the passage of the ADA. This dissatisfaction reflects the concerns of many Americans who failed to find protection against discrimination under other laws. While individual verdicts will certainly depend on the facts of individual cases, the ADA appears poised to provide broad protection against employment discrimination for those who actually carry the HIV virus.

The analysis of the cases presented illustrates a key factor in protecting members of groups at high risk for HIV infection from discrimination. This factor is the presentation of a positive HIV test result or an employee's notification to an employer that he or she is a member of a group in which the incidence of HIV infection has been high. This, however, can clearly backfire on the employee. The sexual orientation of gay men, for example, does not offer protection from discrimination at the federal level and is protected at the state level in only eight states and the District of Columbia. An employee who discloses his sexual orientation to an employer, hoping to find protection under the provisions of the ADA's first definition of a handicap, may leave himself exposed to employment discrimination as section 511(a) of the ADA expressly excludes homosexuality and bisexuality as disabling conditions. An employer is free, in the majority of the fifty states to openly discriminate against homosexuals who receive no protection from state law. Hence, the difficulty of proving under the ADA that someone who may be perceived as carrying the HIV virus when he or she is not is protected from employment discrimination may be significant.

It is noteworthy that the ADA's expanded coverage from the Rehabilitation Act includes people who are simply friends or relatives of those with disabilities. In finding that these individuals are also often discriminated against, Congress included in section 102(b)(4) a provision that prohibits "denying equal jobs or benefits to a qualified individual with whom the qualified disabled individual is known to have a relationship or association." This coverage will help to alleviate the type of discrimination seen in the case of Brunner v. Al Attar, where an employee who volunteered with a Houston AIDS foundation was fired from her job. Her employer was concerned about her developing AIDS and infecting himself, his family, coworkers and customers. The court upheld the firing under Texas law since she did not meet the statutory definition of a handicapped employee and hence had no protection from her employer's action as an at-will employee.

Regardless of the stage of HIV infection in which an individual plaintiff finds him or herself, the establishment of a disability does not automatically guarantee a judgment in favor of the disabled employee. It is critical to keep in mind that the ADA requires disabled individuals to remain "otherwise qualified" to perform their job duties. As discussed, this term defies a measurable, objective definition and such a definition may be contingent upon the nature of the industry and job responsibilities. In determining whether an individual is otherwise qualified, Congress requires the determination to be made at the time of the employment decision and "not be based on the possibility that the employee or applicant will become incapacitated or unqualified in the future." Therefore, in the case of an individual with HIV, decisions regarding hiring and promotion may not consider the likelihood of the future progress of the disease nor rely on past examples of others who have been afflicted.

Even if an individual is judged to be otherwise qualified, the issue of reasonable accommodation presents another potential obstacle. Again, what constitutes a reasonable accommodation will vary from case to case. Although the ADA provides examples of what might constitute such an accommodation, the guidelines are general. Adding to the uncertainty is the fact that employers may refuse to provide such an accommodation if it creates an "undue hardship" for them. The guidelines for undue hardship are vague and need to be determined relative to the specific facts of the case.

The ADA fails to address the key issue of the degree of protection that employees will be offered relative to reduced or discontinued health care benefits. As previously discussed, the ADA grants an exemption from its provision to insurers. While employers have to offer all of their employees the same coverage, they can not be responsible for the decisions of their carriers to unilaterally limit benefits for a particular condition. Now that an increasing number of employers are choosing to self-insure their employees, the provisions of the ADA conflict with the employer's responsibility as both an employer and an insurer. The leading case to date, McGann v. H & H Music, heard under the Rehabilitation Act has allowed employers the latitude to reduce or discontinue health care benefits without liability. Absent further legislation, this practice is likely to be continued.

While the ADA does expressly protect those infected with HIV, the extent of that protection remains to be seen. Until a body of case law is developed under its provisions, the extensions and limitations of its coverage will remain uncertain. While it will take time to develop a systematic, cohesive body of case law, the broad and expanded protection the ADA offers employees with HIV as well as other disabilities makes it probable that there will be increased litigation by employees with disabilities against employers who apparently discriminate.

5

Employer Defenses

Much as employers have found a number of different means by which to discriminate against workers infected with HIV, they have similarly used a number of justifications to defend the allegations against them. The success of these defenses has varied. This chapter presents a categorical analysis of the major defenses employers have utilized in discrimination claims relative to HIV and examines the extent to which the courts have validated or refuted specific defenses and presents the legal justifications for such actions. The objective is to present a systematic model of precedent setting cases concerning specific employer behaviors that allegedly discriminate and to address the legal consequences of these behaviors.

Discussion of Defenses

Employment-at-Will

As previously discussed, the 19th Century doctrine of employment-at-will still governs a significant number of employment relationships today. The only noted exceptions to the doctrine involve 1) violations of laws that establish certain groups in society as "protected classes" or 2) specific terms of a collective bargaining agreement that expressly state agreed-upon terms and conditions of employment.

In addition to this, a number of individual states have recognized exceptions to the employment-at-will doctrine for employee terminations which violate a recognized public policy. The leading case here is Goins v. Ford Motor Company, a Michigan case in which Ford terminated an employee for filing a worker's compensation claim. The court found that the employee had a course of action. Even though the employer, under employment-at-will, had the legal right to dismiss the employee, the Michigan court found the termination to be contrary to public policy and ordered the worker reinstated. The terms of the Employee Retirement Income Security Act (ERISA) later codified the specific issues in the case by prohibiting employers from terminating employees in any attempt to deprive them of benefits to which they were entitled. However, this pre-

ERISA case serves as a model for other claims of terminations that are cited as inconsistent with public policy.

Given the finding in the Goins case, an employee discharged because he or she is infected with the HIV virus could arguably have a claim for wrongful discharge on the grounds that the termination violates public policy. The courts, however, have not found such arguments persuasive and have generally ruled in favor of the employers-at-will. The employment-at-will doctrine was cited as a material fact affecting decisions rendered for employers in several cases.

The court in Petri v. Bank of New York Co., Inc. accepted the bank's argument that Petri was an employee-at-will after establishing the fact that he was not protected by the New York State Human Rights Act. Because Petri had not tested positive for the HIV virus, he could not find protection under the law to constitute a perceived disability. In Chapoton v. Majestic Caterers, the plaintiff who did test HIV-positive was found to not be protected under the Virginia Rights of Persons with Disabilities Act. Even though the court found that the Act applied to symptomatic HIV infection, it also found that Chapoton was an at-will employee.

In the case of Evans v. Kornfeld the court ruled that an HIV-positive employee had no claim under the Pennsylvania Human Relations Act due to his at-will status. The court found that there was no requirement that an at-will employee be terminated for "just cause" and that continued employment opportunities were solely at the discretion of the employer and employee. This court, however, went one step further in specifically rejecting the claim made by the plaintiff that the termination of an HIV-infected employee should be prohibited under the public policy doctrine. The court ruled against this concept in finding the public policy exception of employment-at-will in Pennsylvania not relevant since the discharge had not been motivated by any specific intent by the employer to harm the employee.

In Brunner v. Al Attar, a Texas court also rejected the public policy exception to the employment-at-will doctrine. Brunner, a clerical employee of an auto body and paint shop, was dismissed because she volunteered at an AIDS service organization. The court found that Brunner was an at-will employee, and could be fired for any reason or no reason whatsoever. It further rejected the plaintiff's public policy exception argument in ruling that the Texas Supreme Court had limited public policy exceptions to employment-at-will to two situations: for refusing to perform an illegal act or because the employer attempted to avoid paying an earned pension.

In addition to these cases, there have also been a number of other cases where the courts accepted the employer's defense of employment-at-will. These cases are not cited here because employment-at-will was not the major basis on which the case was decided. The cases already enumerated above clearly illustrate judicial acceptance of the employment-at-will doctrine if the plaintiff is unable to prove that he or she is disabled and that the punitive actions of the employer were based on this disability. Therefore, workers seeking protection under any state public policy exceptions to employment-at-will might find better redress in filing charges under a specific federal or state law. While HIV infection is clearly identified as a protected disability under the Americans With Disabilities Act, the challenge still remains for those who are perceived to be carriers of HIV and discriminated against to find conclusive and consistent support for their claims. It appears questionable, given court decisions to date, that these individuals can find protection under public policy exception arguments to employment-at-will.

Expense to Employer

One common defense employers have utilized to justify discriminating against HIV-infected employees involves the expenses that will be incurred in continuing to employ these workers. The costs relative to anticipated absenteeism and increased health insurance premiums seem to be foremost among employers' concerns. Precedents in non-HIV cases have generally favored the plaintiffs in these claims. In Chrysler Outboard v. Wisconsin Department of Industry, Labor and Human Resources, the employer based its refusal to hire an applicant who had leukemia on anticipated increases in insurance costs and a concern over future absenteeism. The court ruled against the employer. In McDermott v. Xerox Corporation, the court found that higher benefit costs were not justification for refusing to hire an obese applicant. In both cases, the courts further held that the likelihood of future absenteeism was immaterial if the applicant had the capacity at present to perform the job in question. These decisions are consistent with the one rendered in Bentivegna v. United States Department of Labor in which the court rejected the potential long-term health problems as a basis for refusing a diabetic individual a job as a building repair person.

Based on these decisions, the justification for discrimination based on potential costs alone does not appear to be accepted by the courts in the case of HIV. This was indeed the case when the courts heard Shawn v. Legs Company Partnership in which a choreographer filed suit against the production company employing him. Prior to the beginning of rehearsals for the Broadway musical "Legs Diamond," choreographer Michael Shawn was hospitalized with weight loss and high fever and tested positive for HIV. Despite the plaintiff's and his physician's assurances that he would be back at work well before the agreed-to rehearsal start-up date, the producers fired Shawn because they felt they "couldn't risk a $4 million show" should Shawn "break down." Another choreographer was hired even though Shawn was still able to work and had completed all preproduction work on the choreography.

In Doe v. Cooper Investment, the court found that Cooper Investment fired an employee with AIDS to avoid the perceived additional costs which would result from Doe's use of the company health plan. The court found the employer to be in violation of ERISA and issued a temporary restraining order directing Cooper to provide Doe with health insurance. It is important to keep in mind that ERISA prohibits termination based on the denial of health insurance or any other employee welfare benefits.

Some employers, however, have successfully found a way around the arguments presented in these cases. In Alexander v. Choate, the court held that a state may place durational limits on in-patient coverage in state medical plans despite the resulting disproportionate impact on the handicapped as long as the handicapped received equal access to the benefit and the limitation was neutral on its face. Following this reasoning, employers could, therefore, put "neutral ceilings" on benefits packages to insulate themselves from health care costs associated with certain employee conditions, presumably including HIV infection and AIDS.

The courts supported this interpretation twice in two major 1991 cases involving alleged ERISA violations. In the previously discussed McGann v. H & H Music Co., the H & H Music Co. switched its insurance coverage to a self-insurance plan that reduced the cap on AIDS-related benefits from $1 million to $5,000. The court found that the revisions in the employer's insurance coverage were not in violation of ERISA and that the company had the right to change its plan at will. McGann did not have a right to health benefits whose terms never changed. It also found that the reduction of AIDS benefits was not intended to deny benefits to McGann for any reasons that would also not be applicable to other beneficiaries who might then or thereafter have AIDS. Rather the reduction was prompted by the knowledge of McGann's illness and that McGann happened to be the only beneficiary then known to have AIDS. This judgment is consistent with the Supreme Court's decision in Alexander v. Choate.

The same conclusion was reached in the previously discussed case of Owens v. Storehouse, Inc. When the financial condition of the defendant company deteriorated, Storehouse modified its employee health insurance provisions to cap AIDS-related medical benefits at $25,000. The court found no ERISA violation, arguing that ERISA was designed to protect the "employment relationship" and not the integrity of the specific plan. It ruled that ERISA did not provide protection against the modification or elimination of employee benefits accomplished independently of employee termination or harassment.

This case can be contrasted to Doe v. Cooper Investment discussed above in which the plaintiff was terminated. This termination was the key factor affecting the judgment in Doe's favor. The decision in Owens v. Storehouse, Inc. further stated that ERISA allows an employer to consider "business needs" in modifying a plan, justifying the employer's actions from a cost perspective.

Given the facts that ERISA's coverage is limited in preventing employers from discriminating relative to benefits and that the ADA allows insurers an exemption from its provisions, it appears that until the law either is changed or interpreted differently, the employer defense of expense may prevail as long as an employee is not terminated.

Altruistic Concern for Employee

Several employers have attempted to justify their discriminatory treatment of employees infected with HIV by arguing that they were looking out for the employee's best interests in protecting him/her from any further harm. One can speculate that some work environments might lend themselves to this defense much more than others (such as laboratories or other operations with chemicals that might be toxic to those with impaired immune systems, health care environments where germs and disease are prevalent, etc.). However, the courts have demonstrated a reluctance to accept arguments that handicapped or disabled employees or applicants must be terminated or rejected for their own protection.

In the leading employment case involving this defense, Shuttleworth v. Broward County Office of Budget and Management Policy, the court found that the office environment in which Shuttleworth worked posed "no threat whatsoever" to his health. In a non-employment case, the court found in District 27 Community School Board v. Board of Education that the New York City Board of Education had properly allowed a student infected with HIV to attend and remain in a public school even though he showed clinically evident immune suppression but no physical symptoms of AIDS. The court not only found that the school setting involved no risk of casual transmission of the virus to classmates but also that the student's health was not put at risk by exposing his immune system to the classroom environment.

Despite these rulings, a Texas court found in 1991 that an employee diagnosed with ARC was outside of the protection of the Texas Commission of Human Rights Act. In Hilton v. Southwestern Bell Telephone Company, the court found that the plaintiff's condition did not come under the Texas Commission of Human Rights Act's definition of a handicap due to lack of physiological impairment ("the defendant's senses, ability to walk, use his hands and arms, sit or stand are not affected"). It further found him not to be "otherwise qualified" because his job as a drafting clerk would pose "a constant risk of instant death" to Hilton. As noted previously, it found that "the mere act of traveling from home to work and back each day would be death defying" and that "every trip to the pencil sharpener, to the supply closet, to the restroom, to a supervisor's office, or elsewhere—each a job-related function—is a potentially fatal act."

Despite the verdict in the Hilton case, the employer defense of altruistic concern for the employee's well-being appears to be weak and generally not accepted by courts. One need only look at the contradictory reasoning in the Hilton case (it found no impairment while simultaneously finding the ability to travel to work to be "death defying") to realize the flaw in logic and the improbability of any other court utilizing this case as a precedent.

In sum, the only potential acceptance of the defense of altruistic concern might involve one of the specific types of work environments described above or possibly an instance of an employee with more advanced stages of infection who somehow remained "otherwise qualified" and insisted on maintaining his or her position, despite the physical and/or mental demands of work. The first justification was found in Local 1812, American Federation of Government Employees v. Department of State in which the court upheld the right of the employer to deny those with HIV infection certain assignments. In selecting employees for long-term overseas assignments the court agreed that the nature of overseas work preempted the employment of HIV-positive individuals due to the inadequacy of medical care in many foreign countries available to treat the disease.

Relative to the second justification, the court's opinion in Benjamin R. v. Orkin Exterminating Company, Inc. favored limiting the ranks of "otherwise qualified" individuals to those who had not contracted "serious symptoms" of the disease because the presence of symptoms usually makes the individuals "too sick to work" and their debilitated immune systems place them at risk for contracting ailments from their fellow employees.

Fear of Contagion

The single most common justification employers have used for discriminating against employees infected with HIV involves the fear of contagion. This fear has been expressed relative to coworkers, customers or both. It is a generally accepted medical fact that HIV transmission via casual contact is virtually impossible in the workplace. While one might assume that this fear is somewhat irrational now that more is known about HIV (versus what was known ten years ago), all but one of the cases cited involve decisions that were rendered since 1989. Obviously this concern is still compelling.

The courts have consistently cited this medical belief of highly remote possibility of workplace transmission in rejecting defendant pleas for the safety of coworkers of those infected. In Shuttleworth v. Broward County Office of Budget and Management Policy, the court found that Shuttleworth did not have an easily transmitted opportunistic infection at the time of dismissal and that there was no evidence to show that HIV could be transmitted by casual contact at work. In Cain v. Hyatt and Hyatt Legal Services, the court found the employer's perceptions that the plaintiff's AIDS would negatively impact the morale of the staff due to fear of workplace transmission to be "unreasonable fears."

In State of Minnesota v. Di Ma Corporation and Richard Carriveau, Carriveau's, the owner of Di Ma, fears of catching the virus from an employee were considered unjustified. Similarly, in Raytheon Company v. California Fair Employment and Housing Commission, Estate of Chadbourne, Real Party in Interest, the court rejected the defendant's concerns about contagion in denying an employee with AIDS reinstatement. It determined that since HIV is not transmitted through casual contact, the defendant presented no evidence to show the employee to be a risk to his co-workers.

Public school settings, firefighting and health care facilities were also found to be employment settings in which courts ruled in favor of plaintiffs regarding an employer's fear of transmission. In Racine Education Association v. Racine Unified School District, the court found that the school district's policy of placing those with HIV infection on indefinite sick leave constituted illegal discrimination. Once again this was based on the erroneous assumption of possible transmission through casual contact. In Doe v. District of Columbia, the court ruled that the duties of a firefighter posed "no measurable risk" that Doe would infect other firefighters or the public. The court concluded that the risk of Doe transmitting HIV to others could be compared "to that of being struck by a meteor" and that there were no reported cases of transmission by firefighting or emergency personnel through their job duties. In Doe v. Westchester County Medical Center, the court found that in the case of Doe, a hospital pharmacist whose employment offer had been withdrawn, there was a theoretical possibility of HIV transmission. However, this probability was so small as not to be statistically measurable.

Although the courts have generally rejected defendant employer claims of fear of contagion, three rulings have favored the employers. The first of these, Brunner v. Al Attar, was a case in which Brunner, a volunteer with an AIDS service foundation, received no protection because the court found her to not be handicapped. As a result of the fact that the plaintiff was outside of the coverage of the law, the court was not able to address the issue of employer fear of contagion.

The two remaining cases involved health care workers. In the case of

Estate of Behringer v. Medical Center at Princeton the employee, an otolaryngolist and plastic surgeon, had his surgical privileges severely
restricted and later revoked. The court justified the medical center's
actions in finding that restricting the plaintiff's surgical privileges was
substantially justified by a reasonable probability of harm to patients.
This risk of harm included not only actual transmission but the risk of a
surgical accident such as a scalpel cut or needle stick. The court found
that the medical center's policy of restricting the surgical privileges of
health care providers should they pose "any risk of HIV transmission to
the patient" was a "reasonable exercise of the center's authority."

In Leckelt v. Board of Commissioners of Hospital District No. 1 the
plaintiff, an LPN, had job duties that included changing patient's dressings, giving medication both orally and by injection, starting intravenous
lines, performing catherizations, and administering enemas. Leckelt's firing was due to his refusal to provide the hospital with the results of an
HIV test. The court found that because Leckelt's duties involved invasive
procedures and because he failed to comply with hospital policy concerning infectious diseases, he was not otherwise qualified to perform his job
of nurse.

In sum, because transmission of the HIV virus is accomplished only
through the exchange of bodily fluids, most workplaces appear to be
immune from transmission by casual contact. Medical research has
shown that the virus is not transmitted through the air and that it dies
almost immediately upon leaving the human body. Hence, the only
known workplace environments in which the risk of HIV transmission
appears are health care settings.

The United States Centers for Disease Control has published guidelines concerning HIV in the workplace. The guidelines state that
although health care settings did pose some risk of transmission, simple
precautions could reduce that risk to near-zero. These recommendations
were later amended in response to an incident involving an HIV-infected
Florida dentist who allegedly passed the infection on to several patients.
As amended, they state that "infected health care workers who adhere to
"universal precautions" and who do not perform invasive procedures
pose no risk for transmitting HIV to patients." The CDC recommends
that the practice of those health care workers infected with HIV who utilize such precautions should not be restricted.

The universal precautions consist of using gloves and masks and com-
plying with standards for sterilization and disinfection. Those health care
workers who perform exposure-prone procedures are encouraged to
know their HIV antibody status and if infected, encouraged to inform
their prospective patients.

While employers may attempt to justify discriminatory behavior based on a fear of transmission, the courts are unlikely to accept such a defense in a non-health care setting. In health care settings, employers who do not make "reasonable accommodations" of HIV-infected employees relative to these CDC guidelines may find the defense of fear of contagion to be rejected by the courts.

Negative Responses of Customers and/or Coworkers

In several cases employers have justified the firing of HIV-infected employees on the grounds of the objections and/or perceptions of customers or coworkers. This defense is somewhat analogous to cases that arose under the sex discrimination provisions of Title VII of the Civil Rights Act of 1964. Two leading cases heard under that law were decided in favor of the plaintiffs.

In Diaz v. Pan Am World Airways the court held that gender was not a bona fide occupational qualification in the case where an airline carrier argued that competitive pressures brought about by customer preferences required them to hire women rather than men as flight attendants, regardless of the concern that customers would take their business elsewhere. Similarly, in the case of Sprogis v. United Airlines the court held that an employer could not refuse to hire married "stewardesses" because the passengers preferred single ones.

The courts have generally ruled in the plaintiff's favor in cases involving discrimination that had been defended by the rationale of negative responses of others, whether coworkers or customers. In Chalk v. United States District Court, Central District of California, the court ruled in its injunction requiring the Department of Education to reinstate the employee with AIDS to his classroom teaching position that the possibility that the teacher's return to the classroom would produce fear and apprehension in both parents and students was not grounds to deny the injunction. In Isbell v. Poor Richard's, a waiter who was dismissed due to his HIV seropositivity received a judgment in which the court stated that the employer could not rely on the defense of "customer preference" to justify otherwise unlawful discrimination.

A contrary opinion was rendered in the case of Benjamin R. v. Orkin Exterminating Company, Inc.. Although the judgment in this case was for the plaintiff, one judge hearing the case stated in his dissenting opinion that he was unaware of any "reasonable accommodation" that could be made to remedy an employee whose HIV status is of concern to the employer's clients, since "irrational public fear" is "beyond the employer's control." In other words, an employer was not liable for the discriminatory attitudes of behaviors of customers. The judge was implying here that an employer could discriminate against an employee if the employer could prove that the employee's health would cause a loss of business.

A determination of what constitutes a threat versus irrational public fear must presumably take into account the epidemiology of the disease and any breakthroughs in medical research that alter our understanding of such. It appears unlikely that courts might reconsider public fears in assessing how far protection against discrimination should go relative to an employer's legitimate business interests. To date no court has accepted this defense. It would appear that employers have no justification to violate the ADA or any state or local law despite the economic burden that might be placed on them. Much as employers have, in some cases, been mandated by the courts to educate their employees about HIV, a court might realistically require an employer to educate its customers.

Pointless to Hire/Employ a Terminally Ill Person

While it might be expected that a significant number of employment decisions relative to both hiring and promotion of those with HIV might be based on an employee's limited life expectancy, to date only two cases have expressly stated this point as a reason for discrimination. In both of these cases, judgment was rendered for the plaintiff. In Cain v. Hyatt and Hyatt Legal Services, the defendant argued that over time Cain would become incapable of performing his responsibilities. The court, in ruling in the plaintiff's favor, found that Cain's AIDS condition did not substantially interfere with his ability to perform the essential functions of his job. In the case of Shawn v. Legs Production Company, the choreographer initially employed by the production company was seen as a "futile investment" once his HIV test results were made known. In fact, the production company claimed a right to know Shawn's status to avoid "risking a $4 million show."

While there has not been a significant number of cases in which this defense has been utilized, that does not mean that the attitudes on which the defense is based can not motivate other employers to engage in such behavior. However, the terms of the ADA will probably further limit any potential this defense may have for a discrimination allegation. In making a determination of whether or not an employee or prospective employee is "otherwise qualified," the ADA mandates that such determination must be made *at the time of the employment decision* and not be based on speculation regarding an individual's future capabilities. A person infected with HIV who is qualified to perform a job at the time a particular employment decision is made may not be disqualified based on the employer's assumption that the individual may become so ill in the future as to be incapable of performing the job.

This issue of the time factor relative to rendering an individual "otherwise qualified" is an important issue for HIV infection. Because the nature of the disease through its manifestation and remission of symptoms is so random and varies significantly from individual to individual, each case must be decided on its own facts. However, this creates a potential roadblock for the judicial system as an individual's status relative to "otherwise qualified" may change between the time an initial complaint is filed and the time the complaint is eventually heard. It is plausible that someone who is "otherwise qualified" at the time of the complaint may not necessarily be so by the time the complaint is heard. An individual who files a claim requesting injunctive reinstatement who is later unable to remain "otherwise qualified" will gain no benefit from the suit and even though the employer may be found to be in violation of the law, no remedy for the violation would necessarily be provided.

Ignorance

Several employers have attempted to defend their discrimination allegations on the basis that they were unaware of the employee's or applicant's handicap. In order to prove that the alleged discrimination was made on the basis of a handicap or disability, it is necessary to prove that the employer was aware of such a condition to illustrate that the actions taken were a consequence of this condition.

The courts have rendered decisions favoring both plaintiffs and defendants in this regard. Interestingly enough, all of the cases decided in favor of the defendants involved federal law and all of the cases decided in favor of the plaintiff involved state law. Two of the cases involving federal law were also heard at the state level and, in both cases, the state court also decided in the defendant's favor. Nonetheless, an examination of the legal issues and principles affecting the decision may aid in understanding just how far the defense of ignorance can extend.

Leckelt v Board of Commissioners of Hospital District No. 1 was judged in favor of the employer at the federal level as well as at the state level under the Louisiana Civil Rights for Handicapped Persons Act. In this case, the courts found that neither act protected the nurse who was perceived to be infected with HIV because a handicap had not been established. By refusing to provide the hospital with his test results, Leckelt, an LPN with a history of sexually transmitted diseases as well as symptoms of HIV infection, did not establish his protected status, despite his employer's perceptions. This case was also decided based on the fact that the specific nature of Leckelt's duties rendered him not "otherwise qualified" by failing to comply with the hospital's infectious disease control policy.

The case of Phelps v. Field Real Estate Company was also heard under both federal law and state law (the Colorado Anti-Discrimination Act). The case, heard under ERISA at the federal level, involved termination allegedly connected to the costs of insurance benefits. It was judged for the defendant employer with both courts ruling that liability required showing that the employer knew or should have known of the physical condition and the corresponding mandate to accommodate. While the employee had full-blown AIDS, he had not informed his employer and presumably, did not manifest any obvious symptoms of the disease. The rulings stated that there is no liability when an employee prevents the employer from developing an awareness of a handicap.

Ritter v. United States Postal Service was a federal case in which Ritter, a postal worker, was dismissed for chronic absenteeism accompanied by a failure to notify his employer of impending absences. He argued that his absences were due to AIDS and that his dismissal constituted discrimination even though he had not notified the Postal Service of his alleged condition. In ruling for the Postal Service the court found that an employee who asserts a charge of handicap discrimination must show that the alleged discriminant possessed knowledge of the handicapping condition.

While these cases imply that notification of employers of handicaps prior to any alleged discriminatory treatment is necessary to prove a discrimination charge, two state court cases found to the contrary. In the case of State of Minnesota v. Di Ma Corporation and Richard Carriveau, an openly gay salesclerk employed by an adult bookstore was suspected of being infected with HIV. The court ruled under the Minnesota Human Rights Act that even though the defendant did not know the employee's HIV status, the employee was still illegally discriminated against because he was perceived to be carrying the virus.

In Estate of McKinley v. Boston Harbor Hotel, the defendant employer was found to be in violation of the Massachusetts Fair Employment Act. McKinley, a waiter in the defendant employer's hotel dining room, was infected with HIV but never informed his employers. After taking medical leave, he was harassed and reassigned due to the perception that he had AIDS. The perception was confirmed by management's inquiry of McKinley's coworkers as to whether or not they knew if he had AIDS. While the defendant argued that since McKinley never told management about his condition, he was not protected by the statute, the Massachusetts Commission Against Discrimination reached the "inescapable conclusion that the employer did indeed perceive McKinley to have AIDS" and that those perceived to have AIDS were covered under the statute, regardless of the presence or absence of symptoms. It found that employers can not feign ignorance when there are obvious signs of disability and that these perceptions were confirmed by management's questioning of McKinley's coworkers.

While the ADA clearly affords protection to those infected with HIV, two questions remain relative to the defense of ignorance. The first involves an employee who has not notified his or her employer of the infection. In all of the federal cases heard, the courts ruled that ignorance was an acceptable defense for the employer. However, two state laws have been interpreted to imply that the employee is not necessarily required to disclose his or her condition in order to be protected. Because HIV infection is often an "invisible disability" the question remains concerning the role of notification of the employer to insure protection. While employees who do inform their employers of their infection will clearly be protected by the ADA, those who choose not to disclose their HIV infection could find themselves without protection.

The second question that remains to be answered is the validity of ignorance as a defense in cases where employees are perceived to be infected with HIV. While the ADA does include those perceived to be disabled within its coverage, HIV is often an invisible disability, creating a greater potential for the employer defense of ignorance. Further, because HIV infection in men is usually equated with homosexuality, the potential is high for an employer to discriminate against an open or known gay male under the perception that he might be infected with HIV.

As federal law provides no protection against employment discrimination relative to sexual orientation, an employer may legally justify terminating someone perceived to be carrying the HIV virus on the grounds that the employer dislikes gays. If the employee has not tested HIV-positive or if the employee has tested positive and not made this status known, he would have no basis for an employment discrimination claim unless the particular state had passed a law prohibiting discrimination based on sexual orientation. Therefore, in any case in which the defendant employer attempts to use ignorance as a justification for its actions, the deciding factor in the verdict may be the employer's specific actions, as illustrated in the Estate of McKinley case.

Employee Not Protected

One final defense employers have utilized in employment discrimination cases based on HIV involves the argument that the employee is not protected under the applicable law. Employers have had some success in this defense as illustrated in the following cases.

In Rose City Oil v. Missouri Commission on Human Rights, a convenience store employee who was reassigned from sandwich making to cashiering duties and subsequently terminated based on the perception that he was HIV positive found no protection under the Missouri Human Rights Act. In a very narrow reading of the law which specifically included those who were "perceived as being handicapped" as receiving protection, the defendant employer argued that the plaintiff had not established that a handicap existed. The state laws' definition of what constituted a handicap required the *actual existence* of a condition which might be perceived as a handicap. The court concurred stating that perceptions themselves were not actionable unless the accompanying condition existed.

In Petri v. Bank of New York Co., Inc., the plaintiff argued that because the defendant employer knew of his sexual relationship with an HIV-positive man, the bank's action in firing him violated the New York Human Rights Law based on his perceived disability. Bank of New York argued that the plaintiff did not have AIDS nor had he tested positive to constitute perceived disability. The court agreed, finding that the plaintiff had only established the fact that he was a gay male and that mere membership in a high-risk group for HIV would import into the statute a ban on sexual orientation discrimination that the legislature had specifically failed to pass. It found that proof of an illness or the perception of an illness was required as the motivating factor in the firing to make the employer's conduct actionable.

In Leckelt v. Board of Commissioners of Hospital District No. 1 the courts found the LPN not covered by either federal law or the Louisiana Civil Rights for Handicapped Persons Act. The decisions were based on the fact that no HIV test results had been provided by the employee, rendering him unable to claim protected status under either act. As in Petri, the court found that the only thing of which the plaintiff could prove his employer had a specific knowledge, was his sexual orientation, which was not protected under either state or federal law.

In two cases, however, employers who defended their actions on the grounds that the alleging employees were not protected under law had this rationale rejected by the courts. In Shuttleworth v. Broward County Office of Budget and Management Policy the defendant employer argued against the inclusion of the plaintiff's AIDS condition as a protected handicap under the Florida Human Rights Act. The court found that AIDS clearly was "a physical impairment that limited one of more major life activities." In Sanchez v. Lagoudakis the defendant claimed that the plaintiff's allegation of a perceived handicap despite the fact that she tested negative for HIV was erroneous. The court disagreed, finding that the significant issue was the employer's motivation rather than the employee's physical condition. By refusing to allow the employee to continue working until she could prove she was HIV-negative, the court found that "the employer has undertaken the kind of discriminatory action that the (Michigan Handicapper's Civil Rights) Act prohibits."

Employers have had mixed success in utilizing the defense that employees were not protected under relevant laws in their HIV-based employment discrimination claims. It is quite clear in this regard that the ADA expressly includes HIV infection as a disability within the protection it offers. However, as discussed in the preceding section on the defense of ignorance, what remains to be seen is the extent to which employees who have not tested positive for HIV infection or those who have tested positive but have not made their employers aware of this fact will receive protection under the ADA. Again, it can be expected that verdicts may reflect the specific facts of the case but until a cohesive body of case law is developed, it remains to be seen as to whether an employer can justifiably defend the discriminatory treatment of workers perceived to be carrying HIV by arguing that such employees are not protected.

Summary

As evidenced by the above discussion, employers have had some success utilizing specific arguments in defending their discriminatory treatment of workers infected with or perceived to be infected with HIV. The ADA should help to clear up much of the confusion surrounding the issues of whether HIV infection itself is a protected handicap. The important questions concern the coverage afforded to those who are members of high-risk groups who have not tested positive yet may be perceived to be either infected with the virus or be at risk for it, and those who have tested positive but have not disclosed this protected disability status to their employers. These questions have yet to be answered and may be major sources of contention in the courts under the ADA.

The provision of employee welfare benefits is another important issue concerning the ADA and the future of potential claims for discrimination under both the ADA and ERISA. While ERISA does not mandate that employers continue to provide any benefits, including health insurance, to employees, the ADA forbids employers from discriminating against employees with disabilities in all aspects of employment but exempts insurers from such discrimination. The question that remains to be answered is how this law will apply to employers who self-insure their employees. Under ERISA employers have been allowed to legally discriminate against employees in altering or canceling benefits as long as 1) the "employment relationship" continued and 2) the identical terms and conditions were applied to all workers. The extent to which the courts will allow this practice to continue under cases that are heard and argued under the ADA remains to be seen. However, because the terms of the ADA appear so broad in this regard, it appears likely that the courts will not change their interpretations of ERISA under the provision of the ADA. While the decisions rendered in future cases may be logically supported, the fact that Congress has not found a way to resolve this dilemma in employment law may result in increased incidents of such discrimination. A controversy of free enterprise employment may inevitably be turned into a larger problem of public policy through its far-reaching affects on numerous other segments of society.

6

Relationships Between Select Case Variables

As the body of law applied to HIV-related employment discrimination continues to evolve, critical insights can be gained by examining both trends in case law and any relationships that appear to be present or developing within these cases. To explore these trends and investigate the significance of any relationships between variables relating to the cases, nine different sets of variables were paired together and hypotheses were developed and analyzed. While these relationships were not tested for statistical significance due to the overall sample size, they do illustrate some noteworthy trends. A discussion of these relationships as well as their significance and implications follows.

Discussion of Hypotheses

Hypothesis #1

> Ho: Those in more advanced stages of HIV infection are more likely to receive a ruling in their favor.

The first hypothesis involved an investigation of any relationship between HIV status and judgment rendered in the case. A frequency distribution for HIV status is presented in Appendix Table 1 while a frequency distribution for judgment is presented in Table 2. Table 3 presents the actual frequencies observed for HIV status and judgment in a bivariate cross-classification matrix.

In observing the actual frequencies for this data it is evident that the judgment rendered does not appear to be related to HIV status. Regardless of the plaintiffs' state of infection, the courts have seemed to render judgments either in their favor or their employers' at approximately the same frequency as illustrated in Table 3. Jurors and jurists do not appear to be more affected by the symptoms of more advanced HIV-related illness. While it is important to remember that each case has unique facts and has been decided by different individuals, the data show that in general those rendering judgments do not necessarily appear to be overly sympathetic toward those who are more ill.

Hypothesis #2

> Ho: Cases heard under state laws are more likely than cases heard under federal law to result in a ruling favoring the employee.

The second hypothesis involved an investigation of any relationship between level of law and judgment rendered in the case. A frequency distribution for level of law is presented in Appendix Table 4 while a frequency distribution for judgment was presented in Table 2. Table 5 presents the actual frequencies observed for level of law and judgment in a bivariate cross-classification matrix. The data appear to support the hypothesis that state cases are more likely than federal cases to result in a verdict favoring the employee.

In observing the frequencies of the data presented in Table 5, this relationship can be seen a bit more clearly. Cases judged under state handicapped laws tended to favor the plaintiff employee nearly two-thirds of the time while cases judged under federal law favored the defendant employer the majority (approximately 55%) of the time. Given the fact that virtually all of these state laws define a handicapped individual in the same manner as the Vocational Rehabilitation Act, this seems to imply that federal court judges read the law more stringently than state court judges.

The fact that state courts tend to favor the plaintiff employee with greater frequency than federal courts do may be attributable to the increased accountability of the more local courts. Political pressure to support public opinion and protect the disenfranchised may be much more acute at the state level where many judges are elected by the general public and may also aspire to higher level offices or appointments or to long-term political careers. This is in contrast to federal judges who receive life appointments and are only generally dismissed for severe violations of judicial conduct. As a result, federal judges may tend to be less accountable to those who appoint or elect them for their decisions.

However, two caveats are important here. The first of these is that some of the federal cases heard under the Rehabilitation Act were judged for the defendant employer due to a lack of jurisdiction. Lack of jurisdiction generally means that the particular law cited does not cover the employer. The Rehabilitation Act only applies to a small number of employers and several cases, particularly those involving the armed forces, were dismissed due to this lack of jurisdiction. By contrast, state laws tend to have much broader coverage, in most cases, covering nearly all private and public employers in the state.

Initial interpretations of federal law questioned the extent to which HIV infection constituted a handicap more stringently than state laws did. Given that much federal legislation is often the result of a majority of states having passed comparable laws, American legislative history has shown that states often tend to respond to socio-legal issues more quickly than the country as a whole. Federal laws, when passed, also tend to be more vague and general than state laws, requiring more interpretation by the federal judiciary. Many of the state laws have expressly included HIV infection as a handicap or disability whereas this inclusion had to be implied at the federal level. It is not surprising, in this regard that courts hearing cases under state laws have tended to render judgments in favor of the plaintiff more frequently.

A second caveat in this regard concerns the fact that several of the cases heard under federal law were not Rehabilitation Act cases but cases heard under ERISA involving employee health care benefits. ERISA deals with a different set of issues than the Rehabilitation Act does or the ADA will. Unlike the Rehabilitation Act or ADA, ERISA makes broad exceptions for insurers and also clearly allows employers who self-insure employees much more latitude in their conduct toward workers infected with HIV or those having any other disability. Therefore, when interpreting the variation between federal and state law responsiveness to plaintiff claims, the effect that ERISA has on federal responsiveness needs to be considered. Many state laws do not allow the self-insured employer the latitude that ERISA does relative to employer conduct.

Hypothesis #3

> Ho: The more severe the consequences for the plaintiff employee (i.e. termination or denial of benefits vs. reassignment or restrictions on job duties), the more likely the verdict will favor him/her.

The third hypothesis involved an investigation of any relationship between category or type of discrimination and judgment rendered in the case. A frequency distribution for category/type of discrimination is presented in Appendix Table 6 while a frequency distribution for judgment was presented in Table 2. Table 7 presents the actual frequencies observed for type of discrimination and judgment in a bivariate cross-classification matrix. The data appear to support the hypothesis that the more severe the consequences for the plaintiff, the more likely the verdict will favor him/her.

In analyzing the relationship between the two variables the frequency distribution presented in Table 7 shows the data to be somewhat skewed. Because the clear majority of the cases involved termination of the plaintiff, the integrity of the relationship between the variables is clearly questionable. Given that each case has unique facts and all are not based on a consistent application of identical legal principles, the judgment concerning the extent to which this relationship can be deemed to be significant should be reserved until more data is available.

Despite this limitation of the data, one clear trend that is evident is that the only type of discrimination in which the defendant employer is clearly more likely to receive a judgment involves the change in or denial of benefits. This should not be surprising given the above discussion of the protection afforded by ERISA as contrasted to the Rehabilitation Act or state anti-discrimination laws. However, jurists generally appear to be more sympathetic toward those employees who have lost their jobs or benefits as opposed to those who have been reassigned or faced with restrictions on their job duties. One can question whether jurists are generally concerned with these employees' legal rights or are reaching their verdicts by considering the social welfare aspects of HIV. The extent to which jurists are sympathetic to the plight of the employee rather than interested in minimizing reliance on public welfare funds in making these decisions would be an area for future research.

Hypothesis #4

Ho: Commissions and agencies are more likely than judges to render verdicts for employees.

The fourth hypothesis involved an investigation of any relationship between the verdict renderer and judgment in the case. A frequency distribution for verdict renderer is presented in Appendix Table 8 while a frequency distribution for judgement was presented in Table 2. Table 9 presents the actual frequencies observed for verdict renderer and judgment in a bivariate cross-classification matrix. The data appear to support the hypothesis that commissions are agencies are more likely than judges to render verdicts for employees.

In observing the actual frequency distribution data presented in Table 9 for the variables, the relationship between the two variables is quite evident. Cases heard by commissions or agencies have favored the plaintiff 89% of the time while cases involving judges have tended to find more often for the defendant (56% of cases) than for the plaintiff (44% of cases). The reason behind this may have something to do with the venue of law. Given the fact that all of the commissions involved heard cases under state law, this finding might be consistent with the previously discussed premise that state law is more responsive to the needs of a society. It could also be due to the fact that local commissions might feel political pressures to make decisions that are consistent with local public opinion, being responsive to neighbors, friends, and the local business community. Commission members may also have career aspirations that depend on public support.

Hypothesis #5

Ho: Those in more advanced stages of HIV infection are more likely to receive more severe forms of discrimination (i.e. termination or denial of benefits vs. reassignment or restrictions on job duties).

The fifth hypothesis involved an investigation of any relationship between the type of discrimination and HIV status of the plaintiff in the case. A frequency distribution for type of discrimination was presented in Appendix Table 6 while a frequency distribution for HIV status was presented in Table 1. Table 10 presents the actual frequencies observed for type of discrimination and HIV status in a bivariate cross-classification matrix. The data appear to support the hypothesis that those in more advanced stages of HIV infection are likely to receive more severe forms of discrimination.

In analyzing the relationship between the two variables the frequency distribution presented in Table 10 shows the data to be skewed. Because the clear majority of the cases involved termination of the plaintiff, the integrity of the relationship between the variables is clearly questionable and comparison of data values across categories becomes unreliable. Given that the cases have unique facts and are not all based on a consistent application of identical legal principles, the judgment concerning the extent to which this relationship can be deemed to be significant should be reserved until more data is available.

There is, however, one provocative relationship that can be observed in the frequency distribution data. This relationship involves the HIV status of the employee and the percentage of the cases involving termination of the employee. Sixty-nine percent of the discrimination claims by high-risk group members involved termination. Fifty-three percent of the discrimination claims by asymptomatic HIV-positive individuals involved termination. Fifty percent of the discrimination claims by those with ARC involved termination. Finally, 44% of the discrimination claims by those with full-blown AIDS involved termination. This trend illustrates the fact that in the earlier stages of infection or perception of infection, employers are more likely to discriminate by dismissing the employee. As the individual advances to later stages of infection, employers are more likely to utilize other forms of discrimination such as the denial of health insurance benefits. Again, this trend needs to take into account the limited sample size utilized for statistical purposes and examine ongoing and future cases to fully validate the apparent relationship.

Hypothesis #6

> Ho: Judgment is more likely to be rendered for the employer in industries such as health care and food service with a higher *perceived* potential for transmission due to the presence of bodily fluids and fears of food contamination.

The sixth hypothesis involved an investigation of any relationship between the industry of the employer and judgment rendered in the case. A frequency distribution for industry of the employer is presented in Appendix Table 11 while a frequency distribution for judgment rendered was presented in Table 2. Table 12 presents the actual frequencies observed for industry of employer and judgment in a bivariate cross-classification matrix. Only those industries in which six or more cases of discrimination were reported were included. The data appear to support the hypothesis that judgment is more likely to be rendered for the employer in industries with higher *perceived* potential for transmission. Hence, the judgments appear to reflect inaccurate public perceptions and fears about the potential for HIV transmission in certain employment settings.

In analyzing the actual frequency distribution data for this relationship presented in Table 12, the sample size of 37 is quite low for a fifteen cell matrix. Because the number of industries in which HIV-related employment discrimination is so large, it was difficult to group the data in any systematic and logical way by industry. This is evident in that only one cell of fifteen in Table 12 has a value higher than four. Despite the fact that the data do not allow any discernable trends to be identified relative to the relationship of the two variables, one point worth highlighting is the fact that the employers accused of discrimination were found in a wide variety of industries. It is probably not surprising that food service and health care were the primary two industries around which controversies existed concerning the potential for transmission of the virus. Retailing also had a large number of cases, perhaps attributable to large numbers of gay males in the industry. Nonetheless, the wide range of industries represented in the data should illustrate that employment discrimination relative to HIV is not necessarily industry-specific. As the number of cases heard continues to grow, judicial responses by industry would be an interesting area for future research.

Hypothesis #7

> Ho: As time has progressed, it has become more likely that a greater percentage of cases will be judged in favor of the employee.

The seventh hypothesis involved an investigation of any relationship between the year in which the verdict was rendered and judgment in the case. A frequency distribution for the year in which the verdict was rendered is presented in Appendix Table 13 while a frequency distribution for judgment was presented in Table 2. Table 14 presents the actual frequencies observed for year verdict rendered and judgment in a bivariate cross-classification matrix. The data does not appear to support the hypothesis that as time has passed, it has become more likely that a case will be judged for the plaintiff employee.

In analyzing the relationship between the two variables the frequency distribution presented in Table 14 shows the data to be random. Only eight of the twenty-one cells in the matrix have values exceeding two. Hence, the integrity of the relationship is questionable and comparison of data values across categories becomes unreliable. Given that the cases have unique facts and are not all based on a consistent application of identical legal principles, the judgment concerning the extent to which this relationship can be deemed to be significant should be reserved until more data is available.

Nonetheless, the frequency data do show a dramatic trend in cases that were decided between 1989 to 1991. It was assumed in developing the hypothesis that as the epidemic progressed, additional medical evidence would affirm the improbability of workplace transmission and would result in reduced fear and discrimination. It was also assumed that a higher percentage of judgments would be found for the plaintiff employees. However, the trend illustrated in the data is inconsistent with the hypothesis. While plaintiffs received a favorable judgment in 73% of the cases in 1989 and in 53% of the cases in 1990, that figure dropped to 32% in 1991. Again, given the small sample size, the potential for one or two seemingly isolated cases to affect the results is a concern. However, it should be noted that 1990 and 1991 were the years that cases were first heard that related to employee benefits. As judgments in these cases have clearly favored defendants, the trend in this regard may at least be partially attributable to this fact.

This trend could also be attributed to the increased experience of employer counsels in defending discrimination claims. As a greater number of cases have been heard, the presentation of more facts, issues, and legal principles could have allowed these defense attorneys to become much more savvy.

Hypothesis #8

> Ho: Cases heard in the northeastern and far western United States are more likely than cases heard in other areas, particularly the deep South, to favor the employee.

The eighth hypothesis involved an investigation of any relationship between the geographic region in which the case was heard and the judgment rendered in the case. A frequency distribution for the geographic region is presented in Appendix Table 15 while a frequency distribution for judgment was presented in Table 2. Table 16 presents the actual frequencies observed for geographic region and judgment in a bivariate cross-classification matrix. The data appear to support the hypothesis that cases heard in the northeastern and far western United States are more likely to favor the employee than those in other areas.

In analyzing the relationship between the two variables the frequency distribution presented in Table 16 shows the data to be somewhat random. Only three of the thirty-three cells in the matrix have values exceeding three. Hence, the integrity of the relationship is questionable and comparison of data values across categories becomes unreliable. Given that the cases have unique facts and are not all based on a consistent application of identical legal principles, the judgment concerning the extent to which this relationship can be deemed to be significant should be reserved until more data is available.

Despite the questioning of the significance of the relationship of the two variables, the actual frequency distribution data presented in Table 16 clearly shows that Federal Judicial Circuits number 1, 2, and 9 have overwhelmingly favored the plaintiff employee in verdicts rendered. Circuit one consists of Maine, New Hampshire, Massachusetts and Rhode Island, circuit two consists of New York, Connecticut and Vermont, and circuit nine consists of Idaho, Montana, Washington, Oregon, California, Alaska, Hawaii and Nevada. The favoring of plaintiffs in these areas may be indicative of the general reputations both New England/New York and the far West share for liberal ideologies and democratic politics. In fact, five of the eight states that prohibit discrimination based on sexual orientation are within these circuits. These prevailing liberal attitudes often result in more government intervention to protect workers. Hence, state and local laws here are more likely to provide specific inclusion of those infected with HIV infection under disability coverage for employment and other types of discrimination.

At the same time the data shows that cases heard in circuits five and eleven have had judgments that tend to favor the defendant employers. Circuits five and eleven are contiguous with circuit five consisting of Texas, Louisiana, and Mississippi and circuit eleven including Alabama, Georgia, and Florida. As the deep South tends to be the base of conservative ideologies which favor minimal government involvement in the affairs of private enterprise, the trend toward favoring employers in cases heard here is not surprising.

The frequency distribution data also show that there has been a significantly higher number of cases heard in Federal Judicial Circuit number 2 than in any other area. This is not surprising since the district is made up of the states of Vermont, Connecticut and New York. New York has had the highest incidence of HIV infection and full-blown AIDS cases of the fifty states since the epidemic began.

Hypothesis #9

> Ho: When the plaintiff employee is a woman, the verdict is more likely to be issued in her favor.

The ninth hypothesis involved an investigation of any relationship between the gender of the plaintiff and the judgment rendered in the case. A frequency distribution for the gender is presented in Appendix Table 17 while a frequency distribution for judgment rendered was presented in Table 2. Table 18 presents the actual frequencies observed for gender and judgment in a bivariate cross-classification matrix.

It is clearly not possible to reach any valid conclusion concerning this hypothesized relationship as there have been very few cases involving HIV-related employment discrimination of women. If fact, of the 60 cases examined, only three involved a female plaintiff. Hence, as the majority of cases have involved males, no discernable trends can be identified relative to gender. While a significant number of women have been infected with HIV, few cases concerning women have been initiated. It may be assumed that either few HIV-infected women are in the workforce, discrimination is not being directed at them, and/or they are being discriminated against but have failed to file claims against their employers.

The assumption that led to the original hypothesis was that a female plaintiff would not necessarily be as stigmatized as a male. This is due to the fact that many males may presumably be perceived to be gay and suffer from societal prejudice based on their sexual orientation. Women, on the other hand, may be more perceived to be "innocent victims" whose infection is not necessarily due to a "deviant lifestyle." While none of the reported court cases stated the means of HIV infection, it might be interesting for future researchers to examine whether verdicts have tended to favor employees whose infection was not due to "lifestyle" (hemophiliacs, infected health care workers, etc.) more than those whose "lifestyle" was perceived to contribute to infection (gay men, intravenous drug users, sexual partners, etc.).

Summary

The above discussion of hypothesized relationships between variables has some important implications for both plaintiff employees and defendant employers relative to case presentation strategy. Further, some important implications for public policy can be developed from this information. Presented below is a discussion of the implications of each of the hypotheses.

Implications

The test of the first hypothesis shows no relationship between the level of infection and judgment rendered. This hypothesis was designed to investigate whether jurists appear to be more sympathetic when the plaintiff is more ill. Evidently the more advanced, more physically evident symptoms of infection have not swayed jurists. This implies that plaintiff attorney arguments need to focus more on specific case facts and legal reasoning rather than appeals for sympathy to win cases. On the other hand, this finding also has an implication for defense attorneys. As some discrimination claims are eventually settled out-of-court, employer defense attorneys should be less willing to settle out-of-court when the employee is severely impaired under the assumption of sympathetic jurists.

The test of the second hypothesis shows that state cases are more likely than federal cases to favor the employee. As discussed, this may be due to the fact that local judicial agencies are more accountable and face more public scrutiny that federal agencies. The implication here is that plaintiff employees might benefit by filing charges under state and/or local laws when both state/local and federal law have jurisdiction. The analysis shows that this action would increase the probability of success, all other things being equal.

The test of the third hypothesis shows that the more severe the consequences for the plaintiff, the more likely he/she is to receive a favorable verdict. Despite the fact that the first hypothesis shows the failure of jurists to be more sympathetic toward those in more advanced stages of infection, this test shows jurists to be more sympathetic toward those who receive more severe forms of discrimination (such as termination or loss of benefits). This implies that plaintiff attorneys presenting cases with less severe consequences (such as reassignment or restricted job duties) might need to argue more strongly as to the negative effects the employers' actions have had on their clients. This strategy was illustrated in the Shuttleworth case when the court was persuaded that Shuttleworth's reassignment resulted in personal deprivation. On the other hand, this finding shows employers which discriminatory behaviors the courts are less likely to find illegal. Some employers may utilize some of these forms of discrimination in attempts to force employees to resign.

The test of the fourth hypothesis shows that commissions and agencies are more likely than judges to render verdicts for employees. In addition to some of the possible public pressures on state and local officials, these individuals' career aspirations may cause them to make decisions more consistent with perceived public opinion, particularly if they happen to be elected officials. If these conjectures are valid, it might be in a plaintiff's best interest to try to obtain extensive local media coverage of local/state cases to attract heightened public attention. This might make it more difficult for those deciding cases to issue a ruling for an employer. Such a politicized approach could, however, be quite risky. Nonetheless, plaintiff employees appear to have a better chance of prevailing in their cases when arguments are heard by commissions and agencies rather than judges.

The test of the fifth hypothesis shows that those in advanced stages of infection are more likely to receive more severe forms of discrimination (such as termination or loss of benefits). This could easily be attributed to irrational employer fears of a disease with which they remain unfamiliar, implying that employers still need to be educated about HIV infection to calm unfounded fears of contagion. Such action could further be linked to attempts by employers to entice infected employees to resign, thereby protecting the employer's health insurance plan from any perceived exorbitant costs. Employees with HIV infection will never receive complete protection from discrimination in employment until laws are passed that prevent employers from restricting or rescinding health care benefits received by workers.

The test of the sixth hypothesis shows that judgment for defendant employers are more likely in industries with a higher perceived potential for transmission. The obvious conclusion for this is that some judgments reflect inaccurate public perceptions and fears of workplace transmission, implying that judicial education is needed as well as employer education. A judge hearing a discrimination case of an HIV-infected employee may have no more medical knowledge of the disease than a lay person. This further implies that plaintiff attorneys may need to focus heavily on medical facts and testimonies in addition to legal principles and case facts in presenting their arguments.

The test of the seventh hypothesis shows that as time has passed, the likelihood of a judgment for the defendant employer has increased. This has happened in spite of the facts that more has been learned about HIV infection and laws protecting those with disabilities have been ruled to include those with HIV infection. This trend can likely be attributed to the fact that employer's attorneys are becoming more sophisticated in defending discrimination claims. This sophistication can only be a result of experience. Previous cases have established precedents through judicial interpretations of vague statutory terms. These interpretations have presented judgments concerning the extent of the law's coverage as well as exclusions to the law. Therefore these case precedents may be extremely important in the preparation and presentation of arguments. While the facts of every case are certainly unique, both plaintiff and defendant attorneys should closely investigate previous rulings to strengthen their arguments.

The test of the eighth hypothesis shows that geographical variation in deciding cases for either employees or employers has been extensive. Clearly regional political ideologies appear to affect the outcomes of cases. More socially liberal areas that subscribe to increased government intervention to protect workers have provided much more protection to workers infected with HIV than more traditionally conservative areas have under identical or similarly-worded laws. Assuming that these claims are valid, the implication of this is that more specifically-worded state laws are needed in areas like the deep South if discrimination is to be fully eradicated. As this is unlikely to happen in the near future, an additional remedy would be the possible deployment of more experienced federal prosecutors in these areas.

The test of the ninth hypothesis shows that women are no more or less likely than men to receive a favorable judgment. While the number of cases with female plaintiffs was too small to reach any valid and reliable conclusions, a fuller understanding of the law and HIV can be gained by studying the extent to which decisions have significant relationships with lifestyle issues, as previously discussed.

Comment

In assessing the relationships between variables discussed above, it is critical to remember that the cases analyzed within the text most likely represent a fraction of the workplace discrimination actually taking place against those infected with HIV. Incidents handled outside of the courts through union involvement and mediation and arbitration processes are not reported or generally made public. It is reasonable to state that many claims also never make it to the court system and that many who are discriminated against opt against filing complaints. The discussion of trends in this chapter is not meant to be definitive but more advisory for additional investigation.

Further, the cases analyzed herein are each unique with distinguishing facts. An analysis of the relationship between two variables makes the important assumption that the remaining additional variables do not impact the relationship. In many cases this is true but not universally. While a multivariate analysis might be employed to ease this limiting assumption, the population of cases would not lend itself to a valid, reliable analysis. Future research involving a greater number of cases might find multivariate analysis useful in retesting these hypotheses.

Despite these limitations of the analysis utilized in testing certain hypotheses, an examination of both the significant relationships between variables and the frequency distribution data illustrate some important facts. As discussed under specific hypotheses, these insights clearly aid our ability to understand how the law has functioned to date relative to employment discrimination claims based on real or perceived HIV infection. These insights also present a number of important implications for both plaintiff employees and defendant employees relative to case presentation strategy as well as some implications for public policy, which will be discussed in the concluding chapter.

Appendix: Statistical Tables

Table 1
Frequency Distribution—HIV Status
(n = 60)

High-risk group number	9
HIV-Positive (asymptomatic)	27
ARC	5
AIDS	16
--	
volunteer with AIDS organization	1
other	1
not applicable	1

Table 2
Frequency Distribution—Judgment
(n=60)

Employee	32.5
Employer	21.5
Out-of-court settlement	6

Table 3
HIV Status and Judgment—Actual Frequencies

	HIV Status				
Judgment	High-risk Group Member	HIV-positive (asymptomatic)	ARC	AIDS	TOTAL
Employee	5	13	4	8.5	30.5
Employer	3	11	1	5.5	20.5
out-of-court settlement	1	3		2	6
Total	9	27	5	16	57

Table 4
Frequency Distribution—Level of Law
(n = 60)

Federal	18
State	33
Local/Municipal	0

Contract	1
Unavailable	8

Table 5
Level of Law and Judgment—Actual Frequencies

	Level of Law		
Judgment	State	Federal	TOTAL
Employee	21.5	7	28.5
Employer	10.5	10	20.5
out-of-court settlement	1	1	2
Total	33	18	51

Table 6
Frequency Distribution—Type of Discrimination
(n = 77)

Termination	39
Reassignment	11
Denial of or change in benefits	6
Refusal to hire or reinstate	8
Disclosure	4
Harassment	4
Refusal to accommodate	2
Restrictions on job duties	2
Demotion	1

Table 7
Type of Discrimination and Judgment—Actual Frequencies
Type of Discrimination

Judgment	Termination	Denial of or Change in Benefits	Reassignment	Refusal to Hire or Reinstate	Disclosure	Harassment	TOTAL
Employee	21	2	6	4	3	4	40
Employer	14	4	4	2	1		25
Out-of-court settlement	4		1	2			7
Total	39	6	11	8	4	4	72

Table 8
Frequency Distribution—Verdict Renderer
(n = 60)

Judge	33
Jury	3
Commission	18
Arbitrator	1
Not applicable	5

Table 9
Verdict Renderer and Judgment—Actual Frequencies
Verdict Renderer

Judgment	Judge	Jury	Commission/Agency	TOTAL
Employee	14.5	2	16	32.5
Employer	18.5	1	2	21.5
Total	33	3	18	54

Table 10
Type of Discrimination and HIV Status—Actual Frequencies
Type of Discrimination

HIV Status	Termination	Denial of or Change in Benefits	Reassignment	Refusal to Hire or Reinstate	Disclosure	Harassment	TOTAL
High-risk group member	9		2			2	13
HIV-positive (asymptomatic)	16	3	3	4	2	2	30
ARC	3			2	1		6
AIDS	7	2	4	2	1		16
Total	35	5	9	8	4	4	65

Table 11
Frequency Distribution—Industry of Employer
(n = 60)

Food service	11
Health Care	7
Retail	7
Government	6
Financial Services	6
Education	3
Law Firm	2
Public Utility	2
Firefighting	2
Defense	2
Entertainment	2
Hotel	1
Pest Control	1
Auto Body Repair	1
Airline	1
Property Manager	1
Public Transit	1
Unspecified Sales	1
Transportation	1
Travel Agency	1
- - - - - - - - - - - - - - - - -	
Unspecified	1

Table 12
Industry and Judgment—Actual Frequencies
Industry

Judgment	Health Care	Government	Food Service	Retail	Financial Services	TOTAL
Employer	2.5	3	7	4	2	18.5
Employee	3.5	3	3	3	3	15.5
Out-of-court settlement	1		1		1	3
Total	7	6	11	7	6	37

Table 13
Frequency Distribution—Verdict Rendered
(n = 60)

1984	1
1985	0
1986	2
1987	2
1988	10
1989	11
1990	15
1991	11
1992	6
Unavailable	2

Table 14
Year Verdict Rendered and Judgment—Actual Frequencies
Year Verdict Rendered

Judgment:	1986	1987	1988	1989	1990	1991	1992	Total
Employee	2	1	4	8	8	3.5	3	29.5
Employer			4	2	6	7.5	2	21.5
Out-of-court settlement		1	2	1	1		1	6
Total	2	2	10	11	15	11	6	57

Table 15
Frequency Distribution—Geographic Region (Federal Judicial Circuit)
(n = 60)

1	3
2	13
3	3
4	7
5	7
6	3
7	3
8	2
9	7
10	4
11	7
Unavailable	1

Table 16
Geographic Region and Judgment—Actual Frequencies
Federal Judicial Circuit

Judgment	1	2	3	4	5	6	7	8	9	10	11	Total
Employee	3	8	1.5	3	2	2	1	1	6	2	2	31.5
Employer		2	1.5	3	5	1		1	1	2	5	21.5
Out-of-court settlement		3		1			2					6
Total	3	13	3	7	7	3	3	2	7	4	7	59

Table 17
Frequency Distribution—Gender
(n = 60)

Male	56
Female	3
Not applicable	1

Table 18
Gender and Judgment—Actual Frequencies
Gender

Judgment	Male	Female		TOTAL
Employee	29.5	2	2	31.5
Employer	20.5	1	1	21.5
Out-of-court settlement	6			6
Total	56	3	3	59

7

Limitations of Law and Recommendations

While the Americans With Disabilities Act clearly addresses the general issue of employment discrimination against those with HIV infection, despite its good intentions, it has failed to address a number of critical, more specific issues. This chapter will explore the limitations of the ADA and the implications of these limitations. It will also provide some policy recommendations concerning how employers, employees, the courts and the larger society might best deal with HIV-related issues in the workplace.

Limitations and Implications

Employment-at-Will Doctrine

One critical issue that may affect potential future employment discrimination claims relative to HIV involves the employment-at-will doctrine. As has been previously discussed, those who have tested positive for the HIV virus are expressly covered under the terms of the ADA. The first definition of a disabled individual under the ADA also covers those who are perceived to have a disability. The question remains however, as to whether an individual will have to present positive HIV test results to employers in order to receive protection against discrimination.

In two cases in which the employer successfully used the defense of employment-at-will, a court hearing the same case under the ADA would now have to find in the employees' favor. In both Chapoton v. Majestic Caterers and Evans v. Kornfeld the plaintiffs had informed their employers of their HIV seropositivity. The state laws under which these cases were originally heard are now no longer consistent with the ADA, rendering these court decisions baseless as legal precedent.

However, in the case of Brunner v. Al Attar the court held that a volunteer with an AIDS service organization who was fired from her paid employment due to her volunteer activities, was found to be outside of the protection offered under Texas law because she was not handicapped and was an employee-at-will. It should be remembered that in this case the court rejected the public policy exception argument to employment-at-will. Further, in Petri v. Bank of New York Co., Inc., an openly gay plaintiff whose employer had known of his relationship with an HIV-positive man was denied protection because he himself had not tested positive. The court found his dismissal did not violate the law because he was also employed at-will. Therefore, it remains to be seen the extent to which those who have tested positive but have not informed their employer and those who have not tested positive but for some reason may be "at risk" or perceived to be at risk will find protection under the ADA. The courts still must make a determination about the scope of the ADA in actual cases.

Time Consuming/Stressful Judicial Process

The nature of the judicial system can often benefit and penalize both parties. While it guarantees the right to a "fair" trial and allows extensive mechanisms for judicial review through appeal, the completion of this process may often require a tremendous amount of money and time. Individuals with HIV are infected with a lethal virus. Although those with AIDS are living longer, it is still true that those infected with the virus will inevitably die due to the medical complications associated with HIV infection. Time-consuming judicial processes can be quite stressful to the parties involved in the litigation. Those with HIV may be unemployed and without health benefits due to employment discrimination. These individuals may be less able to fight opportunistic illness if involved in stressful and time-consuming judicial proceedings and deprived of health benefits in the interim.

Handicap or disability discrimination law may present a problem in attempting to protect those infected with HIV, particularly those with full-blown AIDS. Potential sanctions of the courts may not be much of a deterrent to employers determined to remove people they perceive to present a health threat to others or those whom the employer simply does not like nor wish to continue to employ. With a case of AIDS, even if a court later orders reinstatement the employee may have died or become so disabled that reinstatement is no longer possible because the employee is no longer "otherwise qualified."

Several cases discussed illustrate this very point, probably none better than Raytheon Company v. California Fair Employment and House Commission, Estate of Chadbourne Real Party in Interest. John Chadbourne, an employee with full-blown AIDS, who had a three-year tenure of consistently high evaluations and maximum available raises, was terminated early in 1984 for his medical condition. He filed a complaint with the California Fair Housing and Employment Commission on April 24, 1984 at which time he was able to perform his job duties without limitation. Chadbourne died in January 1985, before his case was heard. It should be noted here that the court transcripts showed that Raytheon's medical director in this case, had strongly urged the company to "beg for time." The appeal process of the case was finally completed on April 24, 1988, four years to the day of the filing of the initial complaint. The decision in Chadbourne's favor came *more than three years* after his death.

In addition to the Chadbourne case, two other cases had plaintiffs die during the proceedings with the deceased's estates having to continue the suit against the employer. In Estate of McKinley v. Boston Harbor Hotel and Estate of Behringer v. Medical Center at Princeton, decisions were not rendered until well after the plaintiffs' deaths. Both cases took over two years from the time of the filing of the complaint to the rendering of the decisions. In both cases, however, the appellate process had not been exhausted and the threat of the case being dragged out even further remained. In addition to these cases, one can not help but speculate how many individuals who were discriminated against due to their HIV status opted to not pursue actions against their employers due to the expected time factors and/or the potential stress involved.

Cases related to HIV as well as any other life-threatening illness or disability protected by the ADA need to be decided much more expediously. This necessity can be illustrated even more clearly in a non-employment case. In the New York case of Bradley v. Empire Blue Cross the plaintiff, who was in the advanced stages of AIDS, had an identical twin willing to serve as a donor for a bone marrow transplant. The plaintiff's physician estimated that there was a 90% chance of improvement of health and quality of life and an extended life expectancy with the transplant, which would significantly reconstitute the plaintiff's immune system. The plaintiff's insurance company refused to pay for the procedure because it considered the transplant "investigative" despite FDA approval of the operation and the fact that Medicaid funded the same procedure for people it insured. The court found for the plaintiff and mandated that the transplant take place immediately and ordered the insurance company to cover the costs of the procedure. However, during the course of the litigation, the plaintiff developed an eye infection which prevented the transplant surgery. By the time the trial ended, the patient's health had deteriorated so badly that he was no longer a candidate for the surgery. His life expectancy at that point was only a few months.

While an individual with full-blown AIDS often does not survive the protracted litigation, it is also critical to keep in mind that the stress of litigation is also unhealthy for those with HIV infection. Medical experts recommend major lifestyle changes for those with HIV which include a reduction in stress.

The courts are clearly not acting in a timely fashion to remedy discrimination charges. It would appear that special time limitations should be developed to hear cases of terminally ill plaintiffs. Determination of such time limits could be difficult, given variations of symptoms and conditions for different illnesses. However, one state has attempted to remedy this problem.

In response to delays in AIDS-related litigation, New York enacted new procedural rules, effective September 1, 1992, to provide expedited civil trials in cases brought by terminally ill patients. Certification by a physician is required to invoke the provisions providing for speedy pretrial conferences and a sharply circumscribed 90-day discovery period. Trials must commence no later than a year after the complaint is filed.

While efforts such as this are to be applauded, it is questionable whether they are enough. The quality of life of a terminally ill person and his or her dignity are both at stake. Possible interventions include restricting employer defenses and strengthening available remedies for victims in the cases of HIV employment discrimination. Available remedies might include punitive damages and compensatory damages for pain and suffering. Plaintiff's attorneys might also be advised to demand temporary injunctive relief, returning the individual to work pending the outcome of the trial. While this latter procedure may benefit current employees, it becomes more problematic in refusal-to-hire cases. Nonetheless, any streamlining of the judiciary process or means of allowing employees and applicants with HIV infection, particularly those with AIDS, to be and remain employed, benefits not only the employee but also society as the employee will not have to rely on public welfare funds such as unemployment compensation, disability, and/or welfare. While this argument assumes that the plaintiff has a valid claim and will prevail in the judicial proceedings, expedited resolution of claims will be of benefit to both parties even when no discrimination is found.

Vagueness and Adaptability of "Reasonable Accommodation"

The ADA mandates that employers make "reasonable accommodations" to employ workers with disabilities. It lists some previously discussed examples of what the concept might include and further states that reasonable accommodation will depend on the situation. Employers may use the defense of "undue hardship" to deny such accommodation. While the majority of accommodations for disabled workers do not entail a significant expense to the employer, the vagueness of the term and its defenses leave some questions unanswered. Specifically, where are the lines to be drawn in distinguishing a "due" hardship from one that is "undue?" Further, given the unpredictable nature of HIV-related illnesses and the onset and remission of physical symptoms, the adaptability of the application of reasonable accommodation may be difficult to determine.

In the case of Arline v. School Board of Nassau County the United States Supreme Court stated that "a person who poses a significant risk of communicating an infectious disease to others in the workplace will not be otherwise qualified if reasonable accommodation will not remove that risk." Later codified in the Rehabilitation Act, reasonable accommodation was said to include "making existing facilities used by employees readily accessible to and usable by handicapped persons, job restructuring, part-time or modified work schedules, acquisition or modification of equipment or devices, the provision of readers or interpreters, and other similar actions." The Act continued to state that "in determining reasonableness, factors to consider included the size of the employer with respect to the number of employees, number and types of facilities, and size of budget; the type of the employer's operation, including the composition and structure of the employer's workforce; and the nature and cost of the accommodation needed."

It is important to remember that laws are deliberately written utilizing vague terminology. Legislators can not anticipate and are reluctant to cover every single possible contingency. The individual situation and employer and employee needs are critical issues that must be weighted by the courts. Hence, it is not surprising to find that the "vagueness" of reasonable accommodation has meant different things to different courts, despite the fact that the same concept of law was being applied.

Two non-HIV cases illustrate these different interpretations. In Nelson v. Thornburgh, the court required the Pennsylvania Department of Public Welfare to accommodate three blind workers by paying for "readers," sighted individuals who read documents to these blind workers. The blind employees were employed in positions that involved extensive paperwork, and these workers initially had hired such readers at their own expense. Eventually, the employees brought suit under the Rehabilitation Act to force the employer to pay for their readers, the cost of which amounted to $6,638 per year per plaintiff for a half-time reader. The court felt that such costs were "modest" in comparison to the Department of Public Welfare's annual budget of over $300 million.

While Nelson v. Thornburgh appears to present a useful guideline as to what constitutes reasonable accommodation relative to cost, the case of Dexler v. Tisch clouds that finding. In this Rehabilitation Act case a federal court refused to order the United States Postal Service to buy a step stool to accommodate an individual who suffered from "achondroplastic dwarfism." The plaintiff had difficulty extending his arms far enough to efficiently sort mail but argued that, despite this, he remained "otherwise qualified" because he could extend his reach sufficiently by standing on a

$300 step stool. When he asserted that the Postal Service should accommodate his handicap, the court disagreed, finding that the stool was not a reasonable accommodation because it presented safety risks and still would have meant a "loss in efficiency" in the plaintiff's work.

While the Nelson and Dexler cases present different facts, they both illustrate the wide interpretation of reasonable accommodation relative to cost. Because cost is only one measure of the reasonableness of an accommodation, it becomes more difficult to reach an absolute measure of the reasonableness of an accommodation.

Several cases relating to HIV, all heard under the Rehabilitation Act, help to provide some guidelines as to how to interpret reasonable accommodation. In Buckingham v. the United States of America, a Mississippi postal employee who was diagnosed with asymptomatic HIV infection requested a transfer to Los Angeles in order to obtain medical care. When his transfer was refused, he sued under the Rehabilitation Act. The court found that the transfer did constitute a "reasonable accommodation" and awarded the transfer with backpay, full seniority and fringe benefits, and attorney's fees. In Kautz v. Humana Hospital -Lucerne, a surgical technician who was dismissed due to his HIV seropositivity received a judgment from the court because the hospital failed to provide him with reasonable accommodation by offering him another position within the institution.

However, in the case of Leckelt v. Board of Commissioners of Hospital District No. 1, the court found that the plaintiff LPN who failed to comply with hospital infectious disease control policy by providing his HIV status was not covered under the Rehabilitation Act. By failing to report his HIV status to his employer, he prevented the hospital from knowing whether he actually had a handicap that required accommodation. The reason the court upheld the dismissal of the employee was in part due to the fact that the plaintiff had no argument that reasonable accommodation had been denied because no protected handicap had been established. Despite the fact that the plaintiff had an extensive history of sexually transmitted diseases, sexually transmitted diseases are not covered under the Rehabilitation Act.

In the case of Severino v. North Fort Myers Fire Control District, the plaintiff firefighter who was assigned to light duty after testing HIV positive argued that his reassignment violated the Rehabilitation Act. The court held that the reassignment constituted reasonable accommodation in this case because Severino's condition rendered him not "otherwise qualified" to perform the normal duties of a firefighter. The court found that Severino could not perform rescue work, which constituted 90% of an on-line firefighter's duties, without a risk that he might transmit the virus. It should be remembered, however, that in the case of Doe v. District of Columbia the court found that an asymptomatic HIV-infected firefighter was qualified under the Rehabilitation Act to fully perform the duties of a firefighter as there was no "measurable risk" of Doe infecting either other firefighters or the public.

While these cases establish some precedent by shedding some light on what the courts might construe to constitute reasonable accommodation of a worker with HIV infection under the ADA, it is critical to remember that the facts of the case will probably be the overriding force in the verdicts rendered. Indeed, a good deal of the language of the ADA instructs the judiciary to consider the specific facts of the case. In the case of someone with HIV infection employed in a setting where there is no measurable risk of transmission, appropriate accommodations might include flexible scheduling, leaves of absence with or without pay, periodic rest periods, and/or transfer to a new position.

The ADA expressly stipulates that when disabled workers who remain otherwise qualified require reasonable accommodation, the financial burden of such accommodation is a possible mitigating factor to be considered. However, accommodating employees with HIV will probably not require any significant capital expenditure on the part of employers. One further accommodation that has been and might continue to be required by a court would involve AIDS education programs for managers and/or employees, as was required in Estate of McKinley v. Boston Harbor Hotel. Comprehensive education programs designed and delivered by outside agencies generally cost from $300 to $500, a relatively insignificant amount for a large company.

Due to the episodic nature of HIV-related conditions, it will be difficult to apply to HIV the standards set in accommodating other disabilities. As HIV-related illness becomes increasingly debilitating, lessening the individual's stamina and ability to remain productive through a full workday, the overall month-to-month and even week-to-week status of an employee's ability to work can vary substantially. At the same time, the cyclical nature of opportunistic infections can result in periods of improved health. What constitutes reasonable accommodation of an employee with HIV has not been addressed considering the cyclicality and unpredictability of HIV-related illnesses. An accommodation that was initially considered "reasonable" may cease to be so as an employee's condition changes.

Similarly, an employee who is unable to work at a certain point in time, may be able to work periodically or indefinitely at some point in the future. A careful case by case analysis would also therefore require periodic review by employers of both the nature of the employee's condition and the accommodation. In this regard, employers are asked to assume a heavy and relatively unprecedented responsibility in interpreting the "reasonableness" of an accommodation for an employee with a volatile medical condition.

At present, under the ADA, the concept of "reasonable accommodation" of workers with disabilities appears to be defined in static or fixed terms. HIV-related illnesses and conditions require flexible and dynamic criteria relative to the reasonableness of an accommodation. The law has not yet resolved what actions constitute reasonable accommodation nor how changes in an employee's condition affect the reasonableness of ongoing accommodation. The courts will have to deal with these complex issues of worker accommodation as more cases are litigated.

Loss of Protection When Unable to Work

The ADA clearly stipulates that in order to be protected under the Act, a disabled individual must remain "otherwise qualified" to perform the essential functions of his/her job. One issue with which the courts *have* dealt with concerns the extent to which an individual with a communicable disease remains otherwise qualified if there is a risk of transmission to others. The courts have generally accepted the medical opinion that the risk of transmission of HIV in the workplace is virtually nonexistent. This finding invalidates the defense of fear of contagion. However, courts have not systematically addressed the issue of whether an employer can refuse to permit an employee infected with HIV to return to work after a medical leave on the grounds that the employee is no longer otherwise qualified because he or she is a danger to him or herself.

While danger to oneself would probably not be an issue to an asymptomatic HIV-positive employee, an individual who has manifest symptoms of HIV-related illness does become susceptible to a variety of opportunistic infections to which otherwise healthy individuals have immunity. During the flu season, for example, there is a great risk of catching a cold from a coworker. Employees whose immune systems are impaired and whose job duties bring them into contact with a significant number of coworkers may face increased risks to their health. Employers may or may not be able to accommodate these employees. While no cases have been litigated relative to this point, the ADA does allow an employee to be rendered not otherwise qualified if his or her condition presents a danger to others (which is clearly inapplicable to HIV). However, it does not address the unresolved issue of employees being a danger to themselves. Hence, the issue remains as to whether an employee with an impaired immune system might be rendered not to be "otherwise qualified" due to the conditions present in the work setting.

This issue, when placed in a larger context, becomes even more pressing. The ADA requires that disabled employees be "otherwise qualified" and legally protected from discrimination only to the extent that they remain able to carry out the major responsibilities of their jobs. Once the individual loses the ability to perform major job functions, protection ceases. This requirement was first stated explicitly by the United States Supreme Court in Southeastern Community College v. Davis. It severely limits the protection offered against discrimination and was reinforced in a decision rendered in Beauford v. Father Flanagan's Boys' Home. In this case, an employee who became unable to work due to various physical and emotional ailments was discharged and, while provided disability insurance, was denied health and dental benefits as well as the employer's salary continuation program for temporarily disabled employees.

The court of appeals in the case held that the denial of these benefits was not prohibited under the terms of the Rehabilitation Act because Beauford was no longer an "otherwise qualified handicapped individual" within the meaning of the statute. Because she was *unable* to work due to physical and mental impairments, she could not be considered "otherwise qualified," even though she clearly was a handicapped person within the definition of the Act. This case set the precedent that once an employee became unable to work, handicap discrimination law would provide no assistance in securing the work-related benefits specifically designed to assist employees who became unable to work.

The cases heard to date relative to HIV do not shed any light as to how the issue of "otherwise qualified" might affect a plaintiff under the ADA despite the fact that the ADA retains the Rehabilitation Act's language in this regard. In Chalk v. United States District Court, Central District of California, "otherwise qualified" was a major question with which the courts dealt but they limited the context of the transmission of HIV to a classroom setting. Leckelt V. Board of Commissioners of Hospital District No. 1 also dealt with the issue of "otherwise qualified" but in this case, the question involved the plaintiff's failure to follow the employer hospital's infectious disease control policy that rendered him not "otherwise qualified."

The critical issue central to HIV infection concerns employees who are covered under the ADA when they first test positive for the virus. They ultimately lose this protection when they become so ill that they are forced to terminate their employment. While in many cases, employers have continued salary and/or benefits (particularly health insurance), they are not required by law to do so. An amendment to ERISA, the Comprehensive Omnibus Budget Reconciliation Act of 1986 (COBRA), provides terminated employees with the opportunity to continue their group health insurance by paying the premiums themselves at statutory levels. However, many people with HIV-related illness can not afford to take advantage of this because they have simultaneously lost their incomes and other benefits. Currently if disability discrimination law protection ceases entirely when employees' impairments render them unable to work, many persons with disabilities will find little assistance from the ADA or any other law that allegedly protects them. This would, ironically, severely undermine one of the major articulated purposes of such laws as stated in the Rehabilitation Act; to reduce the dependency of handicapped persons on public assistance by providing "independent living."

Relationship of Sexual Orientation to HIV Infection

The majority of reported cases of HIV infection in the United States involve transmission between gay males. Hence, discrimination related to HIV is often intertwined with discrimination based on sexual orientation. While discrimination based on sexual orientation is not outlawed at the federal level, only eight states (California, Minnesota, Wisconsin, Vermont, Massachusetts, Connecticut, New Jersey and Hawaii), the District of Columbia, and a few municipalities have enacted laws prohibiting discrimination in employment on the basis of sexual orientation. Employers have therefore been able to discriminate on the basis of sexual orientation as a way of avoiding employing individuals infected with HIV or perceived to be at risk for HIV. In a significant number of the cases reported, the employer was aware that the plaintiff was a gay male. In most of the cases, however, the plaintiff's sexual orientation was secondary to the fact that he had tested positive for HIV. This point is evidenced in Doe v. Delta Airlines, N. v. A Restaurant, State of Minnesota v. Di Ma Corporation and Richard Carriveau, Evans v. Kornfeld, and Doe v. 315 West 232 Street Corp.

In one state-level HIV case where the state (Wisconsin) has specifically passed a law providing protection from discrimination on the basis of sexual orientation, that fact was cited within the verdict. When a teacher's association challenged its school district's policy of placing employees infected with HIV on disability leave, the teacher's union claimed that the policy was discriminatory. In Racine Education Association v. Racine Unified School District the court found that the policy was based the assumption of possible transmission through casual contact and further found that the policy violated state law prohibiting discrimination based on sexual orientation since the policy's goal was apparently to exclude gay men from teaching positions.

In two other cases, employees who were known to be gay and had not submitted HIV test results were found to be protected by state anti-discrimination statutes. Estate of McKinley v. Boston Harbor Hotel, heard under Massachusetts law, and Connecticut Human Rights Commission v. Respondent both resulted in judgments for the plaintiffs due to the employers' perceptions of HIV infection. In both cases, the plaintiffs' sexual orientation was acknowledged as being a key factor contributing to these perceptions. It is noteworthy that both Massachusetts and Connecticut have laws prohibiting discrimination based on sexual orientation.

Despite the decisions in these two cases, a similar case heard under New York state law was decided differently. In Petri v. Bank of New York Co., Inc., the plaintiff who was known to be gay but who had not presented evidence of HIV infection was not found to be within the protection of the statute. While Petri argued that his employer knew of his sexual relationship with an HIV-positive man, the court found that while the employer knew that the plaintiff was gay, "construing mere membership in a high-risk group as being equivalent to a perceived disability would be to import into the statute a ban on sexual orientation discrimination that the legislature has specifically failed to pass." Hence, while Massachusetts and Connecticut laws have allowed the knowledge of the plaintiff's sexual orientation to be a factor contributing to the perceptions of disability based on HIV, the New York court has ruled differently. This fact clearly supports the assertion that laws prohibiting employment discrimination based on HIV status may be compromised by a corresponding lack of protection of sexual orientation.

The Racine Teachers Association case conclusively shows the protection that can be extended to those perceived to carry the HIV virus under laws protecting discrimination based on sexual orientation. The Petri case clearly illustrates the opposite point of view. Efforts to add protection based on sexual orientation to Title VII of the Civil Rights Act of 1964 have failed in Congress, although the number of legislators in favor of such an amendment has been increasing. At the same time, however, citizens in individual states such as Colorado and Oregon and many municipalities such as Cincinnati and Portland, Maine have voted on referenda to prohibit municipalities from providing any such protection.

As a result, it remains to be seen as to whether under the ADA the fact that an employee is a known homosexual is sufficient to constitute an allegation for employment discrimination based on the perception that the employee is infected with HIV. It is probable that courts would find inquiries about an applicant's or employee's sexual orientation illegal if the purpose were to discover whether a potential or existing employee is at risk for HIV infection. However, to date there are no provisions in any federal law that expressly forbid employers from asking questions concerning sexual orientation. Currently an employer is free to discriminate on the basis of sexual orientation in forty-two states without fear of legal sanction. It is possible that an employer might dismiss an employee or reject an HIV-infected applicant by claiming that the action was motivated by a dislike of gay men. Consequently, any attempt to address the issue of HIV-related discrimination in employment must consider the extent to which such an argument would be acceptable in the absence of a more general ban on sexual orientation-based discrimination.

Loopholes in Insurance Laws

What may be the biggest limitation of employment discrimination law based on HIV or any other disability involves the provisions that apply or fail to apply to insurers. As previously discussed, the courts have ruled that under the Employee Retirement Income Security Act, employers are free to alter or eliminate any employee welfare benefit plans, as long as employees are not terminated or harassed. Judicial application of this provision was previously explained in the discussion of both Owens v. Storehouse, Inc. and McGann v. H & H Music Co.

Funding mechanisms for insurance companies were designed long before the discovery of HIV, hence insurance companies now are being called upon to assume costs that were previously unanticipated. As a result, many insurers have issued new group policies that exclude or cap HIV-related benefits while a number of self-insured companies have even attempted to exclude or limit HIV-related expenses from coverage entirely.

One of the most dramatic examples of this was reported in the *Wall Street Journal* on August 5, 1988. On the previous day, Circle K Corporation, the nation's second largest convenience store chain, had sent a letter to employees announcing a new policy that terminated the medical coverage of employees who became sick or injured as a result of AIDS, alcohol, drug use, or self-inflicted wounds. Circle K, a self-insured company, defended its policy as necessary to protect the benefits of some employees, whom it alleged would unfairly have to subsidize the medical expenses of other employees whose illnesses were due to their "lifestyles." After unwelcome media attention, the company quickly rescinded its policy. However the issue may likely recur in other companies and employers' actions may be in full compliance with the law.

Self-insured employers are not only excluded from ERISA provisions but also have an ERISA pre-emption that prevents state and local governments from regulating the provision of benefits, except for those that violate Title VII of the Civil Rights Act of 1964. In spite of this, some states and municipalities have still attempted to regulate insurers' treatment of those with HIV. These attempts have had very limited success. In American Council of Life Insurance v. District of Columbia, the court upheld a D.C. law that prohibited insurance carriers from refusing coverage, benefits, renewals or changing benefits to individuals testing positive for HIV. The court simultaneously allowed insurers to refuse coverage to those already manifesting symptoms of AIDS. In two other cases, Life Insurance Association of Massachusetts v. Commissioner of

Insurance and Health Insurance Association of America v. Corcoran, the courts denied the power of state insurance commissioners in Massachusetts and New York state to impose similar restrictions on insurers. Both courts further found that using HIV antibody test results as a basis for classifying risks in determining insurability was sound underwriting practice.

The only way around the obstacles presented in ERISA involve claims relative to Title VII of the Civil Rights Act. Because those infected with HIV are not covered under Title VII, they will probably find little relief from discrimination relative to insurance provisions. While in large urban areas, HIV disproportionately impacts persons of color and Hispanic Americans, it is unlikely that discrimination charges based on race, color or national origin would be successful. Likewise, despite the fact that in the United States those infected with HIV are overwhelmingly male, it is unlikely that discrimination charges based on gender would be successful.

One reason for this conclusion is that those infected with HIV are usually sub-groups of protected classes (gay males, drug-addicted members of ethnic groups, etc.). However, in the case of Doe v. Beaverton Nissan & M. F. Slater, Inc. an Oregon court found that the employer's exclusion of HIV-related treatment from the company health insurance coverage violated state law by discriminating against men based on gender. The court reached its decision by reasoning that 90% of those with HIV were male and rejected the defendant's argument that HIV affected only the subgroup of gay males. The court also rejected the defendant's argument that the epidemiology of the disease in Africa indicated that it was not male-specific. Therefore, while significant protection under Title VII appears unlikely, Oregon did set precedent on the state level.

It still remains to be seen as to how one particularly ambiguous section of the ADA will be interpreted by the courts. It is critical to review the exact wording of the ADA to illustrate this ambiguity.

Section 102 of the ADA, which covers employment, states that "No covered entity shall discriminate against a qualified individual with a disability because of the disability of such individual in regard to job application procedures, the hiring, advancement, or discharge of employees, employee compensation, job training, and other terms, conditions, and privileges of employment." It appears that the provision of employee benefits, such as health insurance, might be covered under employee compensation or other "other terms, conditions, and privileges of employment."

However, section 501 (c) states that "Titles I through IV of this Act shall not be construed to prohibit or restrict (1)an insurer...or entity that administers benefit plans... from underwriting risks, classifying risks, or administering such risks that are based on or not inconsistent with state law." While this clearly exempts insurance companies from the provisions of the ADA, the question remains as to how an employer who is also the insurer (a self-insured company) will be affected by the ADA.

Because of this ambiguity, it remains to be seen whether the ADA will be useful to a person infected with HIV who wishes to challenge a discriminatory act by his or her employer/insurer. The courts are also dealing with an important policy issue when weighing the extent to which an employer/insurer is covered under the provisions of the Act that apply to employers rather than those that apply to insurers. The absence of a national health care program in the United States means that without a potential economic compromise on the part of the employer/insurer, health care costs must be born by the individual through private insurance or, in the case of the uninsured, by the state. As most individuals with full-blown AIDS are not able to work, it is unlikely that they will be able to purchase private health insurance unless they have some income replacement. Therefore, in deciding whether to allow employer/insurers to cap or deny health insurance benefits to those with HIV, and particularly to those with AIDS, the courts will also, in part, be deciding whether the health care expenses involved with this care are to be borne directly by the government. It is interesting to note that there have ben very few cases of HIV-related employment discrimination in countries such as Canada and Australia with state-run health care. This absence might be explained by the fact that, with health care costs borne by the state, one discrimination issue important to an both the employer and the affected employee disappears.

Recommendations

Employers

The passage of the ADA has changed how employers must deal with HIV-infected employees. Prior to the ADA, most employers were not explicitly required to accommodate workers with HIV although some did so voluntarily. Now, treating HIV-infected employees fairly is now no longer discretionary. The law levies severe penalties against employers who discriminate. Employers need to curtail discrimination in their workplaces by 1) establishing specific non-discriminatory policies dealing with HIV infection and 2) educating themselves and their employees about HIV.

Policy Recommendations. Employers are advised to establish programs and plans to deal with HIV in the workplace. They can take the initiative by establishing policies that go beyond those simply mandated by law. These policies can and should address hiring, termination, promotions, demotions, transfers, job assignments, and compensation issues. Issues such as "reasonable accommodation" are difficult to put into a blanket policy because each case is unique. However, employers can certainly take the initiative to address other ambiguous issues in the ADA, including health insurance.

An employment policy that encourages employees infected with HIV at any stage of infection to come forward without the fear of being fired or otherwise discriminated against can assist in earlier detection of HIV infection and help to facilitate more manageable and better treatment of the employee's health. To minimize workplace harassment, many employers have instituted employee education programs concerning HIV and found the benefits to far exceed the modest costs.

A proactive approach in addressing HIV at work is clearly in an employer's best interest. Sound workplace policies can impact the "bottom line" by having a positive effect on employee morale as well as by helping the employer avoid costly and often embarrassing litigation, adverse publicity and workplace disruption.

A model example of corporate HIV policy was developed in New England when, in 1989, nine large employers joined together to form the New England Corporate Consortium for AIDS Education. The mission of the consortium has been to provide leadership and advocacy in the business community on workplace HIV issues including education, public policy, community relations, and corporate philanthropy. This consortium, which originally consisted of Bank of Boston Corporation, Bank of New England, Cabot Corporation, DAKA International, Digital Equipment Corporation, Lotus Development Corporation, New England Telephone, Polaroid Corporation, and TEXTRON, developed ten principles for workplace policy relative to HIV. Each of these companies has adopted these principles and the consortium has encouraged several hundred companies nationwide to adopt them as well. These principles are:

1. Persons with HIV infection, including AIDS, in our company have the same rights, responsibilities, and opportunities as others with serious illnesses or disabilities.

2. Our employment policies comply with federal, state, and local laws.

3. Our employment policies are based on the scientific facts that persons with HIV infection, including AIDS, do not cause risk to others in the workplace through ordinary workplace contact.

4. Our management and employee leaders endorse a non-discrimination policy.

5. Special training and equipment will be used when necessary, such as in health care settings, to minimize risks to employees.

6. We will ensure that AIDS education is provided to all of our employees.

7. We will endeavor to ensure that education takes place before AIDS-related incidents occur in our workplace.

8. Confidentiality of persons with HIV infection and AIDS will be protected.

9. We will not screen for HIV as part of pre-employment or workplace physical examinations.

10. We will support these policies through their clear communication to all current and prospective employees.

Education. In order for employers to successfully develop any significant policies regarding HIV infection in the workplace, they must be educated about HIV infection. A large number of cases of employment discrimination resulted from employer ignorance, hostility, or misinformation. This attests to the fact that employers are lacking in knowledge concerning HIV infection. The costs of these cases and the resources wasted in litigation could have been avoided if employers knew more about HIV infection.

In attempting to bring about changes in employer behaviors, it is important to determine how these behaviors are caused. The intention to engage in a behavior is largely a function of two things: the attitudes the individual holds and the individual's perceptions of group and societal norms. Consequently, changes in both employer attitudes and norms will be necessary to change their behavior.

Attitudes toward HIV can be significantly impacted by workplace education programs. Factual information presented from credible sources who have nothing to gain from the intervention are most likely to affect the way people think about HIV disease. Most large urban areas have nonprofit public service agencies that provide workplace HIV education. In addition, the American Red Cross has established its own nationwide AIDS education at work program. Programs such as these have been found to significantly impact employee and employer attitudes concerning HIV infection. The end goal of these education programs is not only to prevent employment discrimination but to destigmatize the disease and promote coworker and employer responses that are more empathetic.

In the early years of the HIV epidemic employers had few role models to turn to upon discovering that an employee was infected with HIV. Many employers panicked because they feared the impact that an infected employee might have on coworkers, customers or operations. Now a large number of major employers have publicized their HIV policies and programs and much of that early reaction has dissipated.

The New England Corporate Consortium for AIDS Education serves as an example for employers nationwide. Ironically, one of the nine members of the consortium is New England Telephone, the defendant employer in the Paul Cronan case. Other large national employers such as IBM, Wells Fargo Bank, Bank of America and Levi Strauss have instituted exemplary standards for other employers to follow. Wells Fargo Bank, Bank of America and Levi Strauss are all based in San Francisco which recorded its 10,000th HIV-related death in January, 1993. Their proactive policies in the very early years of the HIV epidemic reflect the fact that none of these companies has ever had an employee discrimination claim filed. The efforts of these and other companies have been well publicized and send out the important message that HIV education is necessary and desirable in the workplace. These efforts further promote these companies as resources and role models for their colleagues.

Public Policy

Despite the benefits provided by taking a proactive and compassionate approach toward HIV in the workplace, it is likely that many employers will simply follow the letter of the law in their treatment of employees with HIV, much as they do with other legal issues. However, the ADA has some severe limitations in the coverage it provides for workers infected with HIV. The following seven public policy initiatives address this inadequacy and suggest remedies.

Recommendation #1. The first recommendation is that laws and ordinances be passed that allow for more speedy trials and alternative forms of dispute resolution, such as mediation and arbitration. The cases discussed demonstrate the limitation of current laws relative to the time-consuming and stressful judicial process often associated with HIV-related employment discrimination claims. New mechanisms should allow cases to be screened for probable cause of discrimination and, upon the establishment of probable cause, be subjected to stringent time limitations. A judicial process that results in timely resolution of cases creates incentive for employers to avoid discriminatory behavior. It would also allow claims to be settled within a time period that allowed for remedies such as reinstatement if the employee were still able to return to work.

Recommendation #2. The second recommendation is to strengthen existing laws that protect disabled employees. The ADA has a number of loopholes that may allow employers to continue discriminating against workers with HIV. However, while federal laws are binding upon all fifty states, individual states are free to pass more stringent laws as long as these state laws do not violate the corresponding federal laws. Relative to the rights of disabled employees, and particularly those infected with HIV, many states have done just that. In fact, companies located in states such as Massachusetts were basically unaffected by the passage of the ADA because existing Massachusetts state law extended even greater protection to workers with disabilities than the ADA provided. However, many states have failed to pass legislation protecting workers with HIV and other disabilities from employment discrimination. This is illustrated in the discussion of the hypothesis that showed geographical variation in verdicts. The combination of the loopholes and vague terminology within the ADA with limited or no protection at the state level for many employees can easily allow the very form of discrimination Congress sought to eradicate to continue.

There are two ways in which this problem could be addressed. The first is for Congress to amend the ADA and provide even more specific coverage for workers with disabilities. This is unlikely given the facts that federal law is intentionally vague and the ADA is a relatively new law. Congress is unlikely to amend it until it sees some problems with it. The second remedy involves the passage of additional state laws that address the vagueness of the ADA and provide more specific protection to workers infected with HIV. While this has happened in many states, this may not be likely to happen in states in the deep South where protection appears to be most needed. There is a clear regional preference here for minimal government intervention in the affairs of private enterprises. However, these states might be more willing to pass such laws if incentives existed. For example, the federal Department of Health and Human Services could earmark funds for such states for public welfare or health care if such laws were passed. The only way that workers with HIV or any other disability can receive full and uniform protection from discrimination under the law is by passing laws that have consistent and specific terminologies and interpretations.

Recommendation #3. The third recommendation is to strengthen existing laws related to health care coverage. The research presented herein clearly shows that workers with disabilities may have protection against employer actions such as termination, reassignment, and harassment but the law does not ensure their employer-provided health benefits. This was illustrated in the McGann v. H & H Music Co. case. The statistical data also show that denial of benefits is becoming the most prevalent form of discrimination against workers infected with HIV. ERISA provides employees with no protection from loss of health insurance or any other benefits. It is highly questionable as to whether the ADA will provide this protection, given its exclusion of insurers from its coverage.

One remedy for this would be to "vest" employee health insurance benefits. Under vesting, which is required for employer contributions to employee pension funds, employees who are provided with health insurance benefits would be guaranteed retention of the same coverage as long as they remain with their employers. While employers would clearly argue that the cost of such a provision is prohibitive, a compromise could involve exclusions for pre-existing health conditions but require benefits to continue for any treatment that has begun until treatment is completed.

Recommendation #4. A fourth recommendation would be for jurists to insure that the ADA and any other state or local law protecting the disabled address all forms of discrimination. The discussion of the third hypothesis showed that when the employee had less severe consequences from the discriminatory behavior, the verdict was more likely to favor the employer. While it remains to be seen whether this will continue under the ADA, jurists must be reminded that the ADA can not fully protect workers from discrimination unless the more subtle, "less damaging" forms of discrimination are also clearly prohibited by the courts.

Recommendation #5. A fifth recommendation is that the United States Supreme Court hear a case involving employee benefits denial under the ADA. The ambiguity of the ADA requires specific clarification as to how the law is to be interpreted. It is likely that different judges may rule differently as there are yet no precedents to follow under the ADA. Unilateral interpretation of the ADA provided by the high court will be necessary to fully protect disabled workers from discrimination. In a split decision, the Supreme Court refused to hear arguments on appeal in the McGann v. H & H Music Co. case. This refusal can not be repeated under an employee benefits case that comes up under the ADA.

Recommendation #6. A sixth recommendation involves addressing the question of whether the courts have been able to divest the issue of sexual orientation from case facts in deciding HIV-related employment discrimination cases. The analysis of cases shows that those states that protect citizens from workplace discrimination based on sexual orientation tend to have rulings that find for the employee more frequently than states that do not afford this protection. However, the cases reported herein can only serve as anecdotal evidence as to whether discrimination based on sexual orientation affects judgments in HIV employment cases.

Discrimination based on sexual orientation is a much larger social phenomenon, extending to many other aspects of societal behavior and expectation. For that reason, it is recommended that policymakers assess the effect that sexual orientation (and "lifestyle" issues in general) has had on jurists' verdicts. Any relationship between the two would imply that the only way to ensure that those with HIV are not discriminated against would be to pass legislation at the federal level that specifically establishes sexual orientation as a protected class.

Recommendation #7. The seventh recommendation goes beyond the issue of HIV in the court system. It presents a research question that has implications for public policy. Policymakers need to assess the accountability of judges at the federal level. The statistical data illustrate that state and local courts are more likely than federal courts to issue verdicts that favor employees. The tests also showed that commissions and agencies are more likely than judges to render verdicts that favor employees.

One possible explanation for these results is that the court system is not accountable at the level of the federal judiciary. It is obvious that this conclusion can not be reached by looking at one very specialized area of the law such as HIV-related employment discrimination. Nonetheless, the issue clearly has important implications for our legal system, raising a question surrounding the life tenure awarded to federal judges. Does this life tenure and "job security" impede their accountability and responsibility in HIV-related employment discrimination cases and in other areas of law in general?

It is recommended that court decisions be analyzed in this regard in a variety of areas of law to determine 1) how widespread this phenomena is and 2) whether the discrepancy can be attributed to lack of accountability. The results of this further study might imply that life tenure systems be abolished and/or some systematic means of judicial review at the federal level be established.

Summary

The Presidential Commission on the Human Immunodeficiency Virus Epidemic has stated that "HIV-related discrimination is impairing the nation's ability to limit the spread of the epidemic....Public health officials will not be able to gain the confidence and cooperation of those infected individuals or those at high risk for infection if such individuals fear that they will be unable to retain their jobs...and that they will be unable to obtain the medical and support services they need because of discrimination based on a positive HIV antibody test." (Report of the Presidential Commission..., 1989). As courts affirm the rights of defendants, disclosure will likely increase as will earlier treatment and intervention.

Several courts found that the plaintiff's failure to disclose his HIV status to his employer provided grounds for dismissal of a discrimination claim. However, if courts fail to uphold the rights of workers to be free from discrimination in their employment relationships, they will encourage the very behavior Congress has sought to discourage, namely nondisclosure. The provisions of the ADA, in clearly stating that HIV seropositivity is a protected disability, may help significantly in this regard.

Will the ADA Result in More Litigation?

It is possible that the overall number of employment discrimination cases based on HIV could increase or decrease as a consequence of the ADA. An increase could come as the result of three things. The first is the ADA's scope in providing protection to the vast majority of both public and private sector employees in the United States. Employees who had previously been discriminated against who had no recourse under the Rehabilitation Act or state law might now file suit due to the increased protection provided by the ADA.

The second is the fact that the ADA expressly includes HIV infection as a protected handicap. This might make employees and their counsels believe that a lawsuit has a greater potential of being judged in favor of the employee. The pre-ADA ambiguity in the courts concerning whether HIV infection was, in fact, a handicap could have made employees less likely to file a claim.

Finally, people with HIV infection are both living longer and remaining healthy longer. These trends will keep them in the workplace longer, increasing the potential incidence for discrimination.

On the other hand, the ADA could result in a decrease in the number of cases. Because the courts have generally been sympathetic to the majority of plaintiffs in cases where state law expressly included HIV infection as a protected handicap or disability, the fact that the ADA also provides such express inclusion should leave no doubt in employers' minds that any discrimination against those infected with HIV is illegal and actionable. At the same time, carriers of HIV who are living and staying healthier longer than their predecessors may also be more able to withstand the rigors of a trial and the time consuming nature of litigation. This knowledge that employees may have the time and stamina to pursue litigation may deter employers from discriminating.

In this regard ERISA does not prevent employers from discriminating relative to the provision of employee benefits, particularly health insurance benefits, to employees who are not terminated. The ADA's silence on this issue could result in a dramatic increase in the number of discrimination claims related to health insurance benefits. While the overall number of cases concerning employment discrimination in general may decrease, there is a good chance that the number of cases specifically relative to benefits may increase without further legislation.

Epilogue

It is probably safe to say that most employers have not even begun to see the effects of HIV and AIDS in the workplace. Many employers have been able to get away with discrimination largely because employees have become incapacitated and died quickly. In 1982 fewer than 30% of those diagnosed with AIDS lived longer than 18 months. Drugs such as aziodothymidine (AZT) have been found to increase a person with AIDS' chance of survival beyond the traditional 18 month post-diagnosis by more than 100%. New medications and therapies that effectively suppress the advancement of HIV and boost the body's immune system are making it possible for those with HIV infection and particularly full-blown AIDS to continue living and working for longer periods of time. It is clear that the issue of continued employment of those with HIV will become more prevalent in the workplace. In short, while it is not expected that a cure will be found for HIV infection or its related illness in the near future, medical advances are changing HIV infection from a deadly epidemic into a chronic and more manageable disease.

In addition to therapeutic advances, the United States Centers for Disease Control adopted a new definition of AIDS as of January 1, 1992. Under the previous definition, an individual needed to be both HIV-positive and have an opportunistic infection to be diagnosed with AIDS. The new definition does not require such an infection. It only requires that an individual test HIV-positive and have a measure of infection-fighting T cells in the blood below 200 per cubic milliliter (in contrast to the 800-1,000 generally found in healthy individuals).

This change was made because, in its early stages, the illness produces different symptoms in women than doctors were used to looking for in male patients. These symptoms include abnormal pap smears, cervical cancer, chronic yeast infection, pelvic inflammatory disease, irregular or stopped menstruation and early menopause. As a result women have traditionally been diagnosed much later than their male counterparts, effectively cutting them off from earlier intervention that could extend their lives. This change has significantly increased the AIDS census count and brought more individuals, particularly women, under the protection of the ADA. This added protection for women could result in an increase in HIV litigation with female plaintiffs.

Despite the protection the ADA offers individuals infected with HIV, there remain some gaping holes in its coverage, as previously discussed. Until the federal statute is amended, state and municipal laws will continue to be a vital source of protection for many employees, particularly those employed by companies that employ fewer than fifteen workers. Moreso, the ADA is enforced by the Equal Employment Opportunity Commission, which already has jurisdiction over the enforcement of the Civil Rights Act of 1964. This increased responsibility for an already overburdened federal agency may result in slow protracted enforcement of the ADA. Relief may not come quickly or in time for a terminally ill plaintiff.

Given these limitations of federal enforcement activity and the role that aggressive enforcement can play in settling discrimination claims without lengthy litigation, it is expected that state and local agencies will remain at the forefront in the battle against HIV-related employment discrimination. Further developments of state disability law in progressive directions will remain vital. More vital to the fight will be the actions of employers toward their employees infected with HIV. The best way to avoid litigation in the employment of those with HIV is simply for employers not to discriminate. The huge costs in legal fees and human suffering, above and beyond the public health and social consequences and costs of the disease, can easily be avoided. While all society suffers when employers discriminate against employees who carry the HIV virus, those who suffer the most are those who can least afford to do so.

References

Age Discrimination In Employment Act of 1967, P.L. No. 90-202, 81 Stat 603 (1967) as amended 92 Stat 189 (1978).

Alexander v. Choate, 105 S.Ct. 712 (1985).

American Council of Life Insurance v. District of Columbia, 645 F.Supp 84 (Dist. D.C. 1986).

Americans With Disabilities Act of 1989, P. L. No. 101-336, 104 Stat 327 (1990).

Arline v. School Board of Nassau County, 772 F.2d 759 (11th Cir. 1985), cert granted 106 S.Ct. 1633 (1986).

Beauford v. Father Flanagan's Boys' Home, 831 F2d 768 (8th Cir. 1987).

Beavers v. Storehouse, Inc., 18 Pens. Rep. (BNA) 1427, 60 U.S.L.W. 2140 (Aug. 27, 1991) (D. Ga. 1991).

Benjamin R. v. Orkin Exterminating Co., Inc., 390 S.E.2d 814 (W.Va. 1990).

Bentivegna v. U.S. Dept. of Labor, 694 F2d 619 (9th Cir. 1987).

Blendon, R.J. & Donelan, K. (1988). Discrimination Against People With AIDS: The Public's Perspective. *New England Journal of Medicine,* 319, 1022-1026.

Bradley v. Empire Blue Cross, AIDS Litigation Project II 295 (Super. Ct. N.Y. July 31, 1990).

Brunner v. Al Attar, 786 S.W.2d 784 (Tex. App. Houston, 1990).

Buckingham v. United States of America, 1991 WL 57977 (C.D.Cal).

Buler v. Southland Corp., d/b/a Seven-Eleven Stores, et al., AIDS Litigation Project 262 (Super. Ct., Balt. Co, MD January 27, 1989).

Bureau of National Affairs. (1986a). Memo from Assistant Attorney General Cooper On Application of Section 504 of the Rehabilitation Act to Persons With AIDS. *Daily Labor Report,* 122, (June 25, 1986). Washington, D. C.: Buraff Publishing.

Bureau of National Affairs. (1986b). Justice Would Permit Bias By Employers Citing Fear of AIDS. *AIDS Policy & Law,* 1, (July 2, 1986). Washington, D. C.: Buraff Publishing.

Bureau of National Affairs. (1986c). Justice's AIDS Opinion Scored by American Medical Association. *AIDS Policy & Law,* 1, (July 16, 1986). Washington, D. C.: Buraff Publishing.

Bureau of National Affairs. (1988). Justice Department Reverses Itself On Status of AIDS Victims Under Rehabilitation Act. *Daily Labor Report,* 195, (October 7, 1988). Washington, D. C.: Buraff Publishing.

Burgess v. Your House of Raleigh, Inc., 326 N.C. 205, 388 S.E.2d 134 (1990).

Cain v. Hyatt and Hyatt Legal Services, 734 F.Supp. 671 (E.D. Pa. 1990).

Carni v. Metropolitan St. Louis Sewer District, 620 F.2d 672 (8th Cir. 1980).

Chalk v. United States District Court, Central District of California, 840 F.2d 701 (9th Cir. 1988).

Chapoton v. Majestic Caterers, AIDS Litigation Project II 234 (Chancery No. 87-688W, 16 Va. Cir. Ct. for the City of Roanoke, VA, June 7, 1989).

Chrysler Outboard Corp. v. Wisconsin Dept. of Industry, Labor and Human Resources, 13 EPD 11,526, 14 FEP 344 (Wis. Cir. Ct. 1976).

Civil Rights Act of 1964, P. L. No. 88-352, 78 Stat 253 (1964), as amended 86 Stat 103 (1972), 92 Stat 2076 (1978).

Civil Rights Restoration Act of 1987, P. L. No. 100-259, 102 Stat 28 (1988).

Clark v. Prentice Hall, Inc., 233 SE.2d 496 (Ct. App. 1977).

Club Swamp Annex v. Douglas H. White, 561 N.Y.S.2d 609 (A.D. 2 Dept. 1990).

Congressional Record, 134, S256-57 (daily edition January, 28, 1988). Washington, D.C.: United States Government Printing Office.

Congressional Record 134, S5107 (daily edition April 28, 1988). W a s h i n g t o n , D.C.: United States Government Printing Office.

Connecticut Human Rights Commission v. Respondent, AIDS Litigation Project II 226 (Conn. Human Rights Commission No. 86-10215, Sept. 5, 1989).

Cronan v. New England Telephone Co., 41 FEP 1268 (Mass. Super. Ct., Suffolk County, 1986).

Dexler v. Tisch, 660 FSupp 1418 (D. Conn. 1987).

Diaz v. Pan American World Airways, Inc., 3 EPD 8166, F2d 385 (CA-5, 1971), cert. denied 4 EPD 7560, 404 US 950 (1971).

District 27 Community School Board v. Board of Education, 130 Misc 2d 398, 502 NYS 325 (Sup. Ct. 1986).

Doe v. Ball, 725 F.Supp. 1210 (M.D. Fla 1989).

Doe v. Beaverton Nissan & M. F. Salter, Inc., AIDS Litigation Project 258 (Equal Employment Opportunity Commission and Oregon Bureau of Labor and Industry Case No. ST-EM-HP-870108-1353, Oregon Bureau of Labor and Industry, 1986).

Doe v. Centinela Hospital, 57 USLW 2034 (C.D. Cal., June 30 1988).

Doe v. Cooper Investment, 16 Pens. Rep. (BNA) 766 (C.D. Colo. April 18, 1989).

Doe v. Delta Airlines, N.Y. City Human Rights Commission, BNA Daily Labor Report No. 155, August 11, 1992, A-9.

Doe v. District of Columbia, 1992 WL 150704 (D.D.C.), 61 USLW 2022.

Doe v. Garrett, Secretary of the Navy & Harris, Commanding Officer, Naval Air Reserve, Jacksonville, 903 F.2d 1455 (11th Cir. 1990).

Doe v. St. Luke's Hospital, AIDS Litigation Project II 211, (No. 179373 Ohio Ct. of Common Pleas, Cuyahoga Cty. May, 1990).

Doe v. 315 West 232 Street Corp., AIDS Litigation Project 229 (Index No. 17150-1988 Sup. Ct. Bronx Co., NY 1988).

Doe v. Westchester County Medical Center, AIDS Litigation Project II 279, Dept. of HHS, Departmental Appeals Board, Docket No. 91-504-2, Decision No. 191, April 20, 1992.

E. E. Black, Ltd. v. Marshall, 497 FSupp 1088 (D Hawaii 1980).

Estate of Behringer v. Medical Center at Princeton, 249 N.J.Super. 597, (A.D. 2 Dept 1992).

Estate of McKinley v. Boston Harbor Hotel, Mass. Comm. Against Discrimination No. 90-BEM-1263.

Evans v. Kornfeld, AIDS Litigation Project 227 (Court of Common Pleas, Luzerne Co., Penn. No. 3468-C, 1988.

Feinman, J. M. (1976). The Development of the Employment-At-Will Rule. *American Journal of Legal History*, 20, 118-135.

Folz v. Marriott Corp., 594 FSupp 1007 (D.C. Mo., 1984).

Gardner v. Rainbow Lodge, AIDS Litigation Project 238 (No. H-88-1705, U.S.Dist.Ct., Houston Div. S.Dist. Tex.).

Goins v. Ford Motor Company, 347 NW2d 1984 (Mich. Ct. App. 1983).

Gostin, L. (1989). Hospitals, Health Care Professionals and AIDS: The "Right to Know" the Health Status of Professionals and Patients. Maryland Law Review, 48, 12-54.

Gostin, L. (1990). The AIDS Litigation Project. *Journal of the American Medical Association*, 263, 2086-2093.

Gostin, L. & Porter, L. (1991). *AIDS Litigation Project II: A National Survey of Federal, State, and Local Cases Before Courts and Human Rights Commissions.* Washington, D.C.: United States Government Printing Office.

Gostin, L., Porter, L., & Sandomire, H. (1990). *AIDS Litigation Project: A National Survey of Federal, State, and Local Cases Before Courts and Human Rights Commissions.* Washington, D.C.: United States Government Printing Office.

Gottlieb, M. S., Schroft, R., Schnaker, H. M., Weissman, J. D., Fan, P. T., Wolf, A. & Saxon, A. (1981). Pneumocystis Carinii Pneumonia and Muscosal Candidiasis in Previously Healthy Homosexual Men. *New England Journal of Medicine*, 305, 1425-1431.

Health Insurance Association of America v. Corcoran, 551 N.Y.S.2d 615 (A.D. 3 Dept 1990).

Hilton v. Southwestern Bell Telephone Co., 936 F.2d 823 (5th Cir. 1991).

Hummer v. Unemployment Appeals Commission, 573 So.2d 135 (Fla. App 5 Dist. 1991).

Iacono v. Town of Huntington Security Division et. al., AIDS Litigation Project 260 (N.Y.S. Division of Human Rights, 1989).

In Re A., AIDS Litigation Project II 225 (No. GA-0016702039-DN, New York Commission on Human Rights, July 19, 1990).

In Re D., AIDS Litigation Project II 224 (No. GA-0024030987-DN, New York

Commission on Human Rights, Nov. 30, 1989).

Isbell v. Poor Richard's, AIDS Litigation Project 263 (West Virginia Human Rights Commission, Docket No. EH-352-87.

Jensen v. Casa Toltec, AIDS Litigation Project II 222 (Oregon Labor Commission, 1989).

Kautz v. Humana Hospital/Lucerne, AIDS Litigation Project II 289 (No. 04-86-2003, U.S. Dept. of HHS, Office for Civil Rights, AIDS Litigation Reporter, Aug. 25, 1989).

Kohl by Kohl v. Woodhaven Learning Center, 672 FSupp 1226 (W.D. Mo. 1987).

Leader, J. H. (1987). Running From Fear Itself: Analyzing Employment Discrimination Against Persons With AIDS and Other Communicable Diseases Under Section 504 of the Rehabilitation Act of 1973. *Willamette Law Review*, 23, 861-936.

Leckelt v. Board of Commissioners of Hospital District No. 1, 909 F.2d 820 (5th Cir. 1990).

Lemp, G., Payne, S., Neal, D., Temelso, T., & Rutherford, G. W. (1990). Survival Trends for Patients With AIDS. *Journal of the American Medical Association*, 263, 402-406.

Life Insurance Association of Massachusetts v. Commissioner of Insurance, 403 Mass. 410 (1988).

Local 1812, American Federation of Government Employees v. United States Department of State, 662 FSupp 50 (D. D. C. 1987).

McDermott v. Xerox Corp., 65 NY2d 213, 480 NE2d 695, 491 NYS2d 106 (1985).

McGann v. H & H Music Co., 946 F2d 401 (5th Cir 1991), cert. denied 113 S.Ct. 482 (1992).

N. v. A Restaurant, AIDS Litigation Project 270 (NY City Commission on Human Rights, 1989).

National Labor Relations Act of 1935, P. L. No. 74-198, 49 Stat 449 (1935).

Nelson v. Thornburgh, 567 FSupp 369 (E.D. Pa. 1983), aff'd 732 2d 146 (3rd Cir. 1984), cert. denied, 469 US 1188 (1985).

New England Corporate Consortium for AIDS Education (1989). *Responding to AIDS: Ten Principles for the Workplace*. Boston: New England Corporate Consortium for AIDS Education.

"New U.S. Definition of AIDS". *AIDS Law and Litigation Reporter*, October, 1991. University Publishing Group: Frederick, MD. p. 65.

Oil, Chemical & Atomic Workers Local Union No. 6-418 v. National Labor Relations Board, 711 F2d 348 (D.C.Cir. 1983).

Owens v. Storehouse, Inc. 773 F.Supp 414 (N.D. Ga. 1990).

Payne v. Western and Atlantic RA Co. 82 Tenn 507, 1884.

Petri v. Bank of New York Co., Inc., 582 N.Y.S.2d 608 (Sup. 1992).

Phelps v. Field Real Estate Company, Bank Western, Western Capital Investment Corporation, et. al., 57 FEP Cases 1508, 1991 WL 333724 (D. Colo.).

Pregnancy Discrimination In Employment Act of 1978, P. L. No. 95-555, 92 Stat 2076 (1978).

Prewitt v. United States Postal Service, 662 F.2d 292 (5th Cir. 1981).

Racine Education Association v. Racine Unified School District, 476 N.W.2d 707, (Wis. App. 1991).

Raytheon Company v. California Fair Employment and Housing Commission, Estate of Chadbourne, Real Party in Interest, 212 Cal App. 3d 1242, 261 Cal. Rptr. 197 (1989).

Report of the House Committee on the Judiciary, 101st Congress, House Report No. 101-485.

Report of the Presidential Commission on the Human Immunodeficiency Virus Epidemic. (1988). Washington, D. C.: United States Government Printing Office.

Report of the Presidential Commission on the Human Immunodeficiency Virus Epidemic. (1989). Washington, D. C.: United States Government Printing Office.

Rice v. Bloomer, AIDS Litigation Project 244 (U.S.D.C., East.Dist. Va., No. 87-162-A).

Ritter v. United States Postal Service, 37 M.S.P.R. 334.

Rose City Oil Co. v. Missouri Commission on Human Rights, 832 S.W.2d 314, 1992 WL 103027 (Mo.App. 1992).

Sanchez v. Lagoudakis, 1992 WL 197325 (Mich.).

Severino v. North Fort Myers Fire Control District, 935 F.2d 1179 (11th Cir. 1991).

Shawn v. Legs Company Partnership, AIDS Litigation Project II 217 (No. 89-04346, N.Y. Sup. Ct., N.Y. City, AIDS Litigation Reporter May 11, 1990).

Shuttleworth v. Broward County Office of Budget and Management Policy, 639 FSupp 654, 649 FSupp 35 (S. D. Fla. 1986).

Southeastern Community College v. Davis, 442 US 397, 99 S.Ct. 2361 (1979).

Sprogis v. United Air Lines, Inc., 3 EPD 8239, 444 F2d 1194 (CA-7, 1971), cert. denied 4 EPD 7560, 404 US 991 (1971).

State of Minnesota v. Di Ma Corporation & Richard Carriveau, Minnesota Dept. of Human Rights, Dec. 7, 1990.

Sweetland v. Telecheck, Kansas Comm. on Civil Rights, No. 89-C-479, Kan. Dist. Ct., Johnson City, April 28, 1989.

Thomas v. Atascadero Unified School District, 662 FSupp 376 (C. D. Cal. 1987).

Trueman v. Camden et. al., AIDS Litigation Project 237 (Cir. Ct. Wayne Co., Mich. May 16, 1984).

United States Centers for Disease Control (1981). Pneumocystis Pneumonia-Los Angeles. *Morbidity & Mortality Weekly Report, 30,* 250-252.

United States Centers for Disease Control (1985b). Summary: Recommendations for Preventing Transmission of Infection With Human T-Lymphotropic Virus Type III/Lymphadenopathy-Associated Virus In the Workplace.

Morbidity & Mortality Weekly Report, 34, 681-686, 691-695.

United States Centers for Disease Control (1985a). Revision of the Case Definition of Acquired Immunodeficiency Syndrome for National Reporting-United States. *Morbidity & Mortality Weekly Report, 34,* 373-375.

United States Centers for Disease Control (1986b). Summary: Recommendations for Preventing Transmission of Infection With Human T-Lymphotropic Virus Type III/Lymphadenopathy-Associated Virus During Invasive Procedures. *Annals of Internal Medicine, 104,* 824-825.

United States Centers for Disease Control (1986a). Update: Acquired Immune Deficiency Syndrome. *Morbidity & Mortality Weekly Report, 35,* 17-21.

United States Centers for Disease Control (1987). Recommendation for Prevention of Human Immunodeficiency Virus Transmission In Health Care Settings. *Morbidity & Mortality Weekly Report, 36,* 35.

United States Centers for Disease Control (1988). HIV-Related Beliefs, Knowledge, and Behaviors Among High School Students. *Morbidity & Mortality Weekly Report, 37,* 717-721.

United States Centers for Disease Control (1989). Guidelines for prophylaxis against Pneumocystis carinii pneumonia for persons infected with HIV. *Morbidity & Mortality Weekly Report, 38,* 1-9.

United States Centers for Disease Control (1991). Recommendations for reventing Transmission of Human Immunodeficiency Virus and Hepatitis-B Virus to Patients During Exposure-Prone Invasive Procedures, *Morbidity & Mortality Weekly Report, 40,* 1-9.

United States Public Health Service. (1986). Surgeon General's Report on Acquired Immune Deficiency Syndrome. Washington, D. C.: United States Government Printing Office.

United States Public Health Service. (1989). Report of the Surgeon General. Washington, D. C.: United States Government Printing Office.

United States Senate Report No. 1297, 93rd Congress, 2nd Session, 38 (1974).

Vocational Rehabilitation Act of 1973, P. L. No. 93-112, 87 Stat 355 (1973), as amended 92 Stat 2984 (1978).

Table of Cases

Iacono v. Town of Huntington Security Division et. al., AIDS Litigation Project 260 (N.Y.S. Division of Human Rights, 1989), 77

In Re A., AIDS Litigation Project II 225 (No. GA-0016702039-DN, New York Commission on Human Rights, July 19, 1990), 60

In Re D., AIDS Litigation Project II 224 (No. GA-0024030987-DN, New York Commission on Human Rights, Nov. 30, 1989), 74

Isbell v. Poor Richard's, AIDS Litigation Project 263 (West Virginia Human Rights Commission, Docket No. EH-352-87 (1988), 48, 89

Jensen v. Casa Toltec, AIDS Litigation Project II 222 (Oregon Labor Commission, 1989), 74

Kautz v. Humana Hospital/Lucerne, AIDS Litigation Project II 289 (No. 04-86-2003, U.S. Dept. of HHS, Office for Civil Rights, AIDS Litigation Reporter, Aug. 25, 1989), 50, 53, 74-75, 115

Kohl by Kohl v. Woodhaven Learning Center, 672 FSupp 1226 (W.D. Mo. 1987), 32

Leckelt v. Board of Commissioners of Hospital District No. 1, 909 F.2d 820 (5th Cir. 1990), 45-47, 67-68, 75, 88, 91, 94, 115, 118

Life Insurance Association of Massachusetts v. Commissioner of Insurance, 403 Mass. 410 (1988), 122

Local 1812, American Federation of Government Employees v. United States Department of State, 662 FSupp 50 (D. D. C. 1987), 29, 33, 68, 86

McDermott v. Xerox Corp., 65 NY2d 213, 480 NE2d 695, 491 NYS2d 106 (1985), 83

McGann v. H & H Music Co., 946 F2d 401 (5th Cir 1991), cert. denied 113 S.Ct. 481 (1992), 64-65, 71, 80, 84, 121, 128-129

N. v. A Restaurant, AIDS Litigation Project 270 (NY City Commission on Human Rights, 1989), 119

Nelson v. Thornburgh, 567 FSupp 369 (E.D. Pa. 1983), aff'd 732 2d 146 (3rd Cir. 1984), cert. denied, 469 US 1188 (1985), 114-115

Oil, Chemical & Atomic Workers Local Union No. 6-418 v. National Labor Relations Board, 711 F2d 348 (D.C.Cir. 1983), 66

Owens v. Storehouse, Inc. 773 F.Supp 414 (N.D. Ga. 1990), 63-64, 71, 84-85, 121

Payne v. Western and Atlantic RA Co. 82 Tenn 507, (1884), 18

Petri v. Bank of New York Co., Inc., 582 N.Y.S.2d 608 (Sup. 1992), 44, 63, 68, 75, 82, 94, 111, 120

Phelps v. Field Real Estate Company, Bank Western, Western Capital Investment Corporation, et al., 57 FEP Cases 1508, 1991 WL 333724 (D. Colo.), 54-55, 68, 75, 92

Prewitt v. United States Postal Service, 662 F.2d 292 (5th Cir. 1981), 23

Racine Education Association v. Racine Unified School District, 476 N.W.2d 707 (Wis. App. 1991), 77, 87, 119-120

Raytheon Company v. California Fair Employment and Housing Commission, Estate of Chadbourne, Real Party in Interest, 212 Cal App. 3d 1242, 261 Cal. Rptr. 197 (1989), 61, 73, 87, 111-112

Index

152

About the Book and Author

With advances in medicine, more persons with HIV, including those with full-blown AIDS, are able to continue living and working for longer periods of time. This raises serious concerns about ongoing workplace discrimination against these individuals, particularly within the larger context of discrimination against those with disabilities.

In this comprehensive and well-documented analysis, Jeffrey Mello examines how laws intended to protect employees from discrimination have worked or have failed to provide protection for employees with HIV. He analyzes the Americans with Disabilities Act (ADA), looks at key court cases involving the employment rights of those with HIV, and offers important policy recommendations for dealing with the limitations of the ADA.

AIDS and the Law of Workplace Discrimination will be required reading for lawyers, policymakers, scholars of labor law and workplace discrimination, persons with HIV, and HIV activists.

Jeffrey A. Mello is associate professor in the School of Management at Golden Gate University. He received a Ph.D. in law and public policy from Northeastern University, concentrating in employment law. He is an active member of the national and regional divisions of the Academy of Legal Studies in Business, Academy of Management, and Organizational Behavior Teaching Society and has published numerous articles concerning the rights of workers with disabilities.